yummy TODDLER *food*

DINNERTIME
SOS

Also by Amy Palanjian
Busy Little Hands: Food Play!

RODALE
BOOKS

DINNERTIME
SOS

100 SANITY-SAVING MEALS
parents and kids of all ages will actually want to eat

AMY PALANJIAN

Published in the United States by Rodale Books, an
imprint of Random House, a division of Penguin Random
House LLC, New York.
RodaleBooks.com
RandomHouseBooks.com

RODALE and the Plant colophon are registered trade-
marks of Penguin Random House LLC.

Library of Congress Cataloging-in-Publication Data
    Names: Palanjian, Amy, author.
    Title: Yummy Toddler Food Dinnertime SOS /
        Amy Palanjian.
    Description: First edition. | New York : Rodale, [2023]
        | Includes index.
    Identifiers: LCCN 2022025771 (print) | LCCN
        2022025772 (ebook) | ISBN 9780593578506
        (hardcover) | ISBN 9780593578513 (ebook)
    Subjects: LCSH: Dinners and dining. | Quick and easy
        cooking. | LCGFT: Cookbooks.
    Classification: LCC TX737 .P34 2023 (print) | LCC
        TX737 (ebook) | DDC 641.5/4--dc23/eng/20220806
    LC record available at https://lccn.loc.gov/2022025771
    LC ebook record available at https://lccn.loc.gov/
        2022025772

Hardcover ISBN: 978-0-593-57850-6
Ebook ISBN: 978-0-593-57851-3

Printed in Canada
Photographs by Lauren Volo
Cover design by Stephanie Huntwork
Cover photograph by Lauren Volo

10 9 8 7 6 5 4 3 2

First Edition

To Josh, Linden, Tula, and Selway—
for always keeping me company
in the kitchen.

Cheeseburger Bowl,
page 95

CONTENTS

INTRODUCTION

It's the end of the work day. I've finished my day job and am tired from my to-do list, but I'm really looking forward to sharing a meal with my family. Except I'm short on energy to cook, out of patience to chop ingredients, there's a kid hanging on my leg, and I cannot, for the life of me, figure out how to do all the things at once—let alone make a meal that everyone at my table actually wants to eat.

I'm also hungry.

It's enough to make anyone swear off cooking until the kids leave the house.

Feeding a family is hard, sure. But if we can all take a giant step back from the daily barrage of pressure to be perfect that comes from almost everywhere we turn, I think we can find some happiness—or at least a way forward that doesn't immediately feel defeating.

This book is here to help. I've written down every single tip and trick that saves my sanity on a daily basis at dinnertime. These are the recipes that have made it possible for me to make dinner, day in and day out, over the past three years (you know, the years when parenting became even harder than it already was) with fast, reliable meals that my husband and I enjoy as much as our kids do. Okay, sometimes the kids don't love everything, but they like most things and that's a start.

Most recipes in this book take 20 to 30 minutes, if that (or can be thrown into the slow cooker or pressure cooker) because I know that is often the max amount of time we have to get the meal made before everything really falls apart. The ingredients for my recipes are readily available—I tested the majority of the book in a small town where Walmart was my primary store— and there's a focus on minimal chopping and straightforward methods. I fully believe that easier is always the answer, and I ran every single one of these recipes by my family multiple times to ensure they meet that goal. And if you're going to have an ingredient left over after you've made the recipe, I offer ideas on how to easily use it up. (It can be such a waste to have half cartons or cans of ingredients lingering in the fridge.)

I want to share what I've learned in the trenches of "life with kids" to lift some of that dinnertime burden from you. I'll show you exactly how to switch and swap ingredients. I'll demonstrate how to use the ingredients you might have on hand—like chicken in place of fish, couscous instead of rice, beans as a substitute for beef—or to use the ones your family prefers. I'll give you easy ways to add or subtract veggies so you feel confident in tailoring the recipes to your family. I'll provide ideas for how to add flavor while sticking to your food budget, simple tricks to make sure you can enjoy leftovers rather than throwing them away, and know how to feed those "picky" kids without having to make three separate meals to feed your family.

I'm here to remind you that being together is as much a part of dinnertime as anything you cook.

I can't guarantee that you or your kids will love every single recipe in this book—sadly, I am not a wizard!—but I do hope that you learn a few tricks for simplifying what can be a major source of stress for so many families. And, yes, hopefully you'll enjoy your own food along the way too.

These recipes can be served to kids *and* adults—no one should have to cook more than one meal for dinner each night. But the recipes are flexible, so you can adjust for intolerances and allergies and use the ingredients everyone in your family likes most (and that you happen to have in the pantry).

And I know firsthand how little energy we sometimes have to put into dinner at the end of the day, so I did my best to be realistic with prep work, the number of pots and pans that will wind up piled in the sink, and the tools you may require. There is never a need for a food processor, and I will never tell you that this is the easiest meal you've ever had and then start by having you chop three onions, I promise!

That means that my recipes may include some ingredients you don't typically see in a cookbook, such as frozen veggies, precut produce, and store-bought sauces. There can be so much stigma on taking shortcuts, but the truth is that these foods are often just as nutritious frozen as fresh, are often similar (or lower) in price, and, in the case of sauces, are amazing for decreasing the number of other ingredients needed to make a flavorful dish. Some of the recipes are a little more involved—some veggies are impossible to cook without cutting—though I always try to include the option to use a shortcut substitution (like jarred minced garlic or garlic powder, for example). Some days you might have the steam to cook a pot of rice or make homemade chicken tenders from scratch, and other days you may want to buy those items at the store, ready to go. Both options are always welcome and I will never tell you that one is better than the other because I know that one or the other may be better for *you* in the moment.

I also made sure to include a number of recipes that are strictly assembly-only—as in, no actual cooking—or dump-it-all-in-and-cook techniques, whether we're using a sheet pan, a multicooker, or a skillet.

By the way, I'm Amy. Hello!

For almost two decades, I've worked in print and digital media as a magazine editor, a recipe developer, and, more recently, as the creator of the website Yummytoddlerfood.com. I've made it my mission to:

- Help alleviate the giant pile of pressure that families feel about food these days

- Ditch the anxiety about serving "perfect" meals

- Help us remember that kids don't eat the way that charts say they will

- Remind us that it's okay if kids go through phases of likes and dislikes

- Know, way deep down, that no parent needs to cook meals from scratch every single day to be "successful" or "good enough"

It's actually perfectly normal if the kids don't like every single thing you offer them. And meals really are about so much more than the food we serve. I'm here to tell you that it's always okay to do what works best for your family in any phase of life.

My family currently includes me, my husband, and our three kids. I will never tell you that my kids eat everything I make, because they don't. And that's actually not ever my goal. My goal is meals that are happy (i.e., as few tears as possible) and satisfying—where we can connect and catch up and fill our bellies. It's really the only time during the day that all five of us are together without distractions, so the last thing I want to do is be so stressed about cooking or what the kids are eating that I lose sight of that. I want to focus on my own food and to create space for my kids to tune in with their own hunger, fullness, and food preferences. There is so much nutrition pressure out in the world that our table is a safe space for them to explore food, sure, but also to see adults eat a wide variety of food without negative body talk or food-group shaming.

My kids are very opinionated in the kitchen, and they have distinct (and always changing!) preferences, favorite foods, and phases. Feeding them sometimes feels like throwing a dart and hoping it lands on the target, but this is what I expect from three very different people. I encourage my kids to express themselves around food with respect—which often looks like my oldest getting up to grab the ranch dressing for her little brother or my middle kiddo trading the milk that I thought she might want for a cup of ice water. Some days it's my toddler telling me that he's done even though he's only taken a bite. Or my husband adding hot sauce to his food because I never make it spicy enough for his tastes.

All of this usually feels like a work in progress and involves a lot of communication. I want my kids to tell me how I can make a meal yummier. What can we add to make it more appealing to them? What would they prefer for a side dish? (Bonus if they can help me get it to the table!) Which fruit do they want to add to their lunch? I don't believe we need to make all of our kids' favorite foods for each meal and snack of the day, but I do think being responsive to their preferences can improve mealtime dynamics. (And that doesn't mean you need to cut veggies into shapes or make every piece of toast look like it has an owl face.)

I believe that part of my job is to surround my kids with the foods I want them to eat, but also to make sure they feel safe around food. I want them to learn about all sorts of foods—

and to be able to talk about the flavors, textures, and colors of foods—so they can identify (and maybe even enjoy) them when they are out in the world without me. I don't care if they eat the broccoli today, but I sure want them to know what it is so they can feel confident on that day in the future when they do decide to give it a go.

It's been interesting to have them go off to daycare and school and learn to eat a much wider range of food. I am grateful for those experiences (and eternally thankful for lunches and snacks provided by schools and childcare centers). One kid has discovered that she actually likes tomato soup when it's paired with grilled cheese. Another decided that yogurt can be really yummy when it's layered with fruit and cereal in a parfait. And the third knows that peas aren't his favorite, but he can eat around them and still have a satisfying lunch.

My kids are constantly around (and underfoot) in the kitchen and, sometimes, they even cook with me—but almost never on a weeknight. We do it when we have time and when I'm not feeling anxious about the extra steps it will take to get through the process. Having them involved in the process is one way that I help them become more comfortable with foods, even if they aren't ready to eat them yet. They (again, sometimes) help wash produce, chop it with kid-safe knives, and even make parts of dinner. This ebbs and flows. We don't do it when we have a lot going on, but I want them to be comfortable with basic kitchen tasks as they continue to grow.

You'll notice as you read this book that the way I talk about food with my kids, and in my recipes, is a little different. I don't push nutrition because I don't think it serves the bigger picture of our own relationship with food and the one that's developing in our kids. I like to call foods what they are—as in, "This is broccoli" or "This is a chocolate chip cookie." I don't use words like "healthy," which means so many different things to different people and is all too often used to get us to eat more of some foods than others (with a side of guilt). I try to explain actual flavors and textures using words such as "crispy," "sweet," "chewy," and more, and I compare new foods with ones they know better. So they have usable information.

Focusing so much on "healthy food" can quickly turn into pressure, power struggles, and parents trying to do everything we can to "get the kids to eat." That distracts us from being able to enjoy our time together—and it's certainly not helping anyone relax at the table and actually eat.

I want to make sure that every person in my family has enough food at each meal to feel safe. That we are able to drop our worry about what each person is or isn't eating so we can focus on being together. That the food I make to share with my family tastes really good. That does not mean that I don't care about nutrition. I just care about the context in which we're eating, cooking, and sharing food.

A Note About Dinner

Somehow, dinner has become the meal that we're told matters most to share with the kids, the one where we get the most pressure about what meals should look like. But it's also the one that is the hardest to pull off, logistically speaking. Our culture has set us up to fail before we even set foot in the kitchen!

In reality, this is the time of the day when our kids may be the most tired, when they want our attention, and when we are burned out on energy. It's also the meal where we often expect our kids to eat more challenging foods—dinner usually has more veggies and more new foods than breakfast and lunch, which can quickly turn this meal into a stressful time for everyone. But if you can recognize some of these external factors that make this feel so hard, we can look at ways to make things easier.

One thing that has helped me a lot in this is to dismiss the worry about how much my kids eat. Which means that I never try to "get them" to eat more of any one food or another, ask them to taste bites of certain foods, or particularly care if they eat a lot or not a lot at that meal. We know that they will eat if they are hungry. And while that may not always work for kids with feeding differences or challenging family relationships, or those with medical issues that make feeling hunger a challenge, every family benefits from trusting their kid's bodies. And it gives us space to have conversations about our days . . . without getting bogged down in the minutia of who's eating what. (Some kids may benefit from reminders to taste new foods. My kids immediately bristle at even a whiff of being told what to do, so we don't do that in our house. Do what works best for your family and doesn't add stress.)

I know that my kids thrive on routine and often eat better if they are free from pressure, so we try to explain what's on the table as needed and then talk about all sorts of other things. The easiest way that I know to help the kids eat more of the foods I've offered is to simply let them do it on their own terms. (And once our oldest turned five, jokes became a mainstay of our dinner table, so there's hardly space for food talk now anyway!)

Ultimate Family
Charcuterie Board,
page 86

Tikka Masala Chicken &
Cauliflower, page 176

There are nights when my kids are hungrier than I expect, and we have to add a simple bedtime snack. And there are others when the youngest one takes a sip of milk and is done. I have learned that sometimes I'm a little off in my estimate of their appetite level—so I let them show me how hungry they are by starting with small portions and keeping seconds at the ready in the middle of the table. Because just as I would feel very uncomfortable if anyone else presumed to know my personal hunger level, I respect that in my kids, too, and try to let them have that bodily autonomy.

Dinner is just another meal. It's a time to refuel and to connect if we all happen to be able to be at the table together. It is not a chance for me to measure my worth or success, to judge how well I'm raising the kids by how much broccoli they eat. What the kids eat or don't eat should never be taken as a judgment on *your* parenting, either. And we don't have to let the food we buy, decide to cook, or prefer to eat define our value. Food can just be *food*—satisfying, comforting, safe, and delicious.

How I Cook

I often remind people that because cooking is my job, I don't always cook like a "normal" person. I frequently spend the day making recipes for work or shooting videos for social media and then transition to making dinner for my family. But because my kids are regular kids—and are often splitting my focus and asking for things while I'm trying to make a meal—I know full well how challenging it is to cook for a family when so much else is going on.

This may sound backward, but most nights, I try to start with an idea of what *I* want to eat. I have learned over the years that the biggest factor in my ability to keep serving meals day after day is to make sure that I get to eat the food that I love as much as my family does. I love big salads (particularly a big chopped salad), vegetarian pastas, and simple soups. So I make those regularly and add to them to ensure my family has food they prefer too. That means the salad has some chicken or shrimp and toasted bread on the side, I serve the spaghetti with a pair of kid-safe scissors so my little guy can cut his up himself, the soup may have a base of veggies but also some sausage for my meat-loving husband, and there are plenty of noodles in the mix for the kids.

Women, in particular, tend to put kids and partners first, and while I know it can be hard to center our needs, it can go a long way toward helping us feel more included and *seen* in the middle of often chaotic mealtimes. So I keep my desires front of mind and *then* factor in the preferences of the kids. (At lunchtime, the kids more regularly see their favorite foods, like mac and cheese from a box, and I can easily make myself a turkey sandwich.) From there, I keep meals streamlined with the help of shortcut pantry staples. I use a lot of jars of marinara and pizza sauce and cans of beans. And I rely on prepped foods from the store, like frozen veggies and bagged lettuces and salad kits to help me save time. I made all of those foods from scratch before I had kids, but I let go of that expectation and pressure as life became busier.

I also try to be realistic about the energy I'll have at 5:30 p.m. and what else may be going on. I think nothing of subbing in "Sandwich Night" or tapping my husband to make bean and cheese quesadillas.

Most nights, I make a main dish and surround it with no-cook sides, like diced fruit, toasted bread with butter or jam, or applesauce. Occasionally on the weekend—or when we have family over—we do more elaborate cooking. All of this is to say, I don't spend all day planning or making dinner—I don't do it during the week and I don't set aside a chunk of a day on the weekend to do it either. If it works for you to take that approach, great—have at it! If the thought of meal prepping instead of playing with the kids or taking a nap makes you start to sweat, let it go. There is so much room for us to do things our own way.

Fifteen-Minute Flatbread Pizza, page 126

My Favorite Food Essentials

Since becoming a parent, I've lived in a house where we used two shelves in a small cabinet as our "pantry," and in another house with a walk-in pantry that has more shelving than we could ever need. I've had a spacious freezer and one with a giant ice-maker that took up all the space.

The things that I keep on hand haven't really changed, though, especially since my main goal with pantry and fridge staples is to keep a supply of the foods that I know my family uses regularly. This helps with food waste—nothing goes unused for too long—and allows me to make quick meals from what I have. My personal favorite staples include a collection of "whole" ingredients such as rice, lentils, plain yogurt, and cheeses along with "shortcut" ones, like jarred marinara sauce, simmer sauces, pesto, frozen veggies, and canned beans and tomatoes. Plus, all kinds of pasta. That mix allows me to cook filling and flavorful meals without needing to cook entirely from scratch every day.

There is so much variation between what's available to each of us where we shop, but my favorites should be readily available at regular grocery stores and big-box stores. I almost never have all of these at any one time—and I'm certainly not saying that anyone else needs to have them all either—but I want to share my go-to items for stocking up.

IN THE PANTRY

Bread crumbs: I like to use regular, Italian-seasoned, and panko (which is crunchier when baked as a coating on fish or chicken).

Canned beans: Black beans, garbanzo beans, and white beans are my favorites.

Canned coconut milk: Both light and regular have more flavor than cartons of coconut milk sold in the dairy aisle and are used frequently in Thai and Indian dishes.

Canned crushed tomatoes: I use regular and fire-roasted ones.

Chicken stock: I reach for the reduced-sodium stock so I have more say over the saltiness, or I sub in vegetable stock as needed.

Coconut oil: Refined or unrefined work similarly. This subtle flavor is a nice pair for Thai- and Indian-style recipes.

Enchilada sauce: Green or red mild enchilada sauce is flavorful and so much easier to buy than to make it from scratch.

Grains: Farro, quinoa, and assorted rice varieties are affordable, rich in fiber, and an easy base for all types of dishes.

Lentils: Brown and red lentils are vegetarian proteins that cook quickly and are receptive to many flavors.

Marinara sauce: I use this for pasta, yes, but also to add flavor to soups and stews and to poach meat and fish.

Noodles: Egg noodles, rice noodles, ramen noodles, soba noodles, and more are delicious and an easy way to make homemade versions of foods we commonly buy as takeout.

Nuts and seeds: Salted peanuts, slivered almonds, and roasted sunflower seeds can enhance the flavor and texture of many dishes (and are a yummy snack on their own).

Olive oil: I use extra-virgin olive oil for a neutral, light flavor.

Olives: Black and Greek-style olives can add flavor to dishes, from bowls and salads to pasta and bakes.

Pasta: Spaghetti, pastina, rigatoni, orzo, lasagna—there are a lot of options for different recipes and preferences.

Pesto: From a container or jar, it's a cost-effective way to add flavor and nutrients to pasta, pizza, and more.

Pizza sauce: Jarred or canned pizza sauce is packed with flavor and obviously great on pizza and pizza toast. It can also be used as a warm dip.

Salsa: Mild salsa is full of flavor and means you don't need quite as many spices in some Mexican dishes. I usually buy a smooth variety as I like how it easily blends into recipes.

Thai-style red curry sauce: Paired with coconut milk, this is a simple shortcut to getting Thai flavors at home.

Tikka masala simmer sauce: I love this for poaching chicken, shrimp, tofu, and chickpeas, as it imparts instant Indian flavor.

Tomato sauce: Whether "no salt added" or enhanced with herbs and spices, tomato sauce provides an inexpensive way to add robust flavor to soups, stews, chilis, and pasta dishes.

Tortillas: Corn, flour, and alternative-grain tortillas are useful to keep on hand for wraps, quesadillas, burritos, and more. The usual sizes are fajita (6 inches), taco (8 inches), and burrito (10 inches).

Whole-grain crackers: These are a perfect side to add to soups or salads. And if kids don't love the main dish, crackers can become a meal for them when paired with cheese and cucumbers.

IN THE FRIDGE

Bouillon paste: This is intensely flavored and often a much less expensive option than buying box after box of store-bought stock.

Cheese: Shredded, sliced, or grated, it adds flavor, calcium, and protein. I prefer grated Parmesan from the dairy aisle rather than shredded or shelf-stable grated in the canister, as I find it has the most flavor. Or look for Pecorino Romano to save a little money as it is often less expensive than Parmesan.

Eggs: One of the more inexpensive and quick-cooking protein options, eggs are a go-to for easy dinners. Buy whichever kind you prefer!

Greek yogurt: Plain yogurt works as a dip or topping for a range of foods and can double as a simple side for the kids. I prefer whole-milk yogurt for flavor, creaminess, and fat content.

Hummus: Prepared hummus can be thinned into a dressing or served as a spread, dip, or topping. Brands vary widely, so try a few to find a favorite.

Lemons: A little fresh grated lemon zest or juice can brighten up a soup or pasta dish.

Limes: Limes are a great way to accent dishes, like curries, with extra zing.

Minced garlic: If even the idea of mincing fresh garlic is too much, buy a jar that's ready to go; the few dollars are more than worth it for ease of use.

Salad kits: Caesar salad kits have been the gateway salad for my kids. Any variety of kit can form the base of a satisfying meal, although store brands may be less expensive.

Soy sauce: I prefer reduced-sodium soy sauce but use tamari if it needs to be gluten-free.

Teriyaki sauce: I know you can make this at home, but you can buy a bottle of reduced-sodium sauce from the store for less than the cost of buying all the ingredients . . . and it usually tastes a lot better too.

Toasted sesame oil: This has so much flavor, and a bottle will last in the fridge for months.

Tzatziki sauce: Topping Greek-style tacos, hummus bowls, and more, this yogurt-based sauce feels fancy, but it's often readily available in stores.

Italian Sausage with
Broccoli & Potatoes,
page 125

Lemon-Chicken Noodle
Soup, page 217

IN THE FREEZER

Fish & shellfish: Stock up on fish sticks, shrimp, and tilapia.

Ginger: Store a whole fresh knob in a freezer bag in the freezer so it never goes bad. Then grate it (still frozen, peel and all) on a Microplane grater as you need it.

Meat: I like to keep Italian sausage, ground beef, chicken tenders, chicken thighs, and breakfast sausage at the ready.

Pesto: I store leftover pesto in a freezer bag, pressed flat so I can easily break off as much as I need each time. I add frozen pieces to hot pasta, and it melts right in.

Potatoes: Hash browns, diced sweet potatoes, and french fries are easier to cook quickly when they're already prepped.

Veggies: I try to keep mixed veggies, minced onion, broccoli florets, cauliflower "rice," sweet corn, and peas on hand.

Whole-grain bread: I like to have sandwich bread, Italian-style bread, flatbread (such as lavash), pita bread, or naan at my fingertips.

ON THE SPICE RACK

Chili powder: This isn't actually spicy, so it's a flavorful addition to Mexican-style dishes.

Cinnamon: Yes, cinnamon is a baking staple, but it's also helpful in bringing out flavors in North African and Morroccan dishes.

Cumin: I love using ground cumin in tacos, burritos, and Greek-style and other dishes.

Dried oregano: A little of this goes a long way to add flavor to Italian dishes but also to basics, like Sloppy Joes.

Dried rosemary: I like to crush this a little with my fingers so the pieces are finer in the finished dish.

Garam masala: This spice is worth having as it's packed with that flavor you expect from Indian-style chicken.

Garlic powder: I often use this in place of fresh garlic in recipes; the flavor is different but similar.

Onion powder: Whenever I don't have interest in chopping a whole onion, this is my go-to.

Paprika: In this cookbook, if you see me call for paprika, plan to use the sweet version.

Pizza seasoning: A sprinkle of this herb-spice mixture adds classic pizza flavor in an instant.

Salt: I use fine sea salt. If you use a different type, you may need to taste and adjust as needed.

Taco seasoning: You can make your own taco seasoning mix, but you can also just pick up one that's ready to go; I prefer the latter option since it's easier!

Indispensable Kitchen Gear

We moved recently, so I took careful stock of what I had in my kitchen and noted what I actually used all the time. These are my kitchen essentials. As you'll see, my list isn't that long. I really try to limit single-use gadgets and tools. This keeps my drawers and cabinets clutter-free so the items I do use regularly are quite accessible.

IN THE CUPBOARD

Baking sheets: In my sheet-pan recipes, I use a standard half-sheet pan. If you have a smaller oven, use two quarter-sheet pans instead. I like the ones with little raised lines, which help prevent food from sticking. I coat sheets well with nonstick spray or olive oil or line with parchment paper to make cleanup easier.

Cutting board: A big cutting board is an essential that we often overlook in the kitchen. Go bigger than you think you need so you always have the space necessary for food prep.

Deep sauté pan with lid: A 12-inch-deep sauté pan or frying pan with a lid can help make one-pot or skillet meals doable, even if you have a larger family to feed. Stainless steel is a great material for this basic pan.

Electric griddle: Once we had our third kid, we added an affordable electric griddle to our kitchen to more easily make larger amounts of quesadillas, grilled cheese, and pancakes. (I was so resistant to the idea of this since I thought it would take up too much space, but we use it all the time!) The surface is much larger than a pan so you can cook more food at once, and it heats up almost instantly.

Kitchen scissors: I use scissors for cutting raw meat right into the pot or pan (no need to dirty the cutting board!); cutting off sandwich crusts; cutting up broccoli, oranges, waffles, and more. Really, a good pair of kitchen scissors is essential to feeding a family. I use scissors so much more than any knife I own. They also eliminate the need for any other fancy chopping devices—and should last you for years. I've been using the same pair for over a decade.

Microfiber kitchen towels: A few years ago, I treated myself by tossing all my old cotton towels and investing in a stash of microfiber ones. They are so much more effective for cleaning up spills and drying produce since they absorb so much liquid. They also last through endless washings and dryings.

Microplane: I use a fine Microplane grater to grate frozen ginger and fresh lemon and lime zest right into recipes, which is a quick way to add flavor to food with minimal work.

Multicooker: The type of pressure cooker, slow cooker, or multicooker you have is often a matter of personal preference, but you can make recipes written for one or the other work with what you have. I particularly love this for soups, chili, and tender meats, like shredded chicken.

Nonstick pans: I love my nonstick pans for cooking delicate foods, like eggs, without worry. As long as the pans are cared for, unscratched, and used according to the manufacturer's recommendations (which usually means over low to medium heat, rather than high), they are a safe and easy way to cook. You can also use a well-seasoned cast-iron pan if you prefer.

Reusable storage bags: Whether plastic or silicone, storage bags make it a breeze to save and keep leftovers in the pantry, fridge, and freezer. I have a stash of silicone ones that I use regularly—and, thankfully, they're easy to clean and dry on the drying rack.

Sharp knives: There are three knives that I use in my kitchen—a basic large chef's knife, which I use mostly for cutting veggies; a small paring knife, for quickly cutting fruit; and a serrated knife, for cutting foods such as bread and tomatoes. I really ignore all others.

Soup pot (4- to 6-quart): This big pot is an essential in my kitchen for making pasta and soups. I love stainless-steel pots in this size with well-fitting lids.

Storage containers: Ever since I had kids, my fridge has been filled with small glass jars with colorful lids. And, honestly, they are really helpful for storing any amount of foods and snacks. From there, we size up to glass and plastic containers to hold leftovers and for packing lunches.

On Making the Most of Leftovers

There are people who love leftovers and those who don't. I fall somewhere in the middle, usually hoping that my husband just eats them all. (Ha!) But I have learned that there are ways to make leftovers a lot more appealing and have found time-saving methods for making some of our favorite staples in bulk and purposefully saving them for future use.

Most leftovers can be stored in the fridge in an airtight container for up to five days. And, generally, you can simply warm them in the microwave in short increments of about 30 seconds, stirring as needed, until evenly heated through. (You can also warm soups or anything in a sauce, really, in a small pot on the stove over low heat. Just stir often to help the mixture warm evenly and to avoid burning and keep the food from sticking to the pot.)

You can heat foods that were crispy the first time around, like chicken tenders, on a baking sheet in a 375°F oven for 6 to 8 minutes to get them back to that same texture. This works similarly whether the food was in the fridge or freezer. (In an air fryer, do the same 375°F, but decrease the time to about 4 minutes.)

Fish can be trickier to reheat since it's so delicate and does not take well to overcooking. Be very, very gentle if warming leftover fish and heat for just 15 seconds at a time, stopping to check the temperature with your finger.

You can also freeze foods such as meatballs, soups, pasta sauces, pesto, chicken, enchiladas, and more by transferring to a freezer container or bag, removing as much air as possible, and freezing for up to 6 months. Thaw overnight in the fridge and heat as desired.

Pasta, if frozen, may be softer when reheated than the first time around. You can do it, though!

You may want to change up how you serve leftovers to make them more appealing—if that's needed with any particular food. For example, soups can be offered as a sauce for grains or as a

Red Lentil–Coconut
Soup, page 222

dip for crackers or chips if the kids prefer it that way. Top pasta with a different type of cheese or sprinkle shredded cheese on top and pop under the broiler to melt and brown. Cooked chicken, beef, fish, or shrimp can be served over a salad. Small bits of leftovers can turn into a sort of shared tapas plate.

And if I'm ever cooking foods such as rice, beans, shredded chicken, quesadillas, or burritos from scratch, I always try to make twice as much so I can freeze half, since I know my family will use those leftovers in future weeks.

Easy Ways to Add Flavor to Food

If any of these recipes don't have enough flavor for you—or you just prefer more heat and spice than the kids—here are some go-to toppings to enhance your own plate:

- **Coarse sea salt or kosher salt**
- **Crushed red pepper**
- **Fresh lemon or lime juice or zest**
- **Fried eggs**
- **Hot sauce**
- **Minced fresh herbs (such as cilantro, basil, and parsley)**
- **Pickled jarred vegetables (such as red onion or jalapeños)**
- **Plain Greek yogurt or sour cream**
- **Pomegranate molasses**
- **Reduced-sodium soy sauce**

Tips for Special Diets

TODDLER TIP

When feeding younger toddlers or older babies, use a pair of kitchen scissors to quickly cut up food into very small or thin pieces for easy eating. Avoid whole nuts, grapes, cherry tomatoes, or very crunchy chips, crackers, or raw produce (like big chunks of carrots or apples) for kids under age 4 as these can be choking hazards. When in doubt, matchstick-size pieces of raw produce—so very thin strips—are usually safer and easier for little kids to eat. And always make sure the kids are sitting down and positioned upright, rather than running around or reclining, for safety too.

I know that many families are dealing with either a food allergy, intolerance, or preference these days that can make it hard to cook one meal for everyone at the table—or to cook from someone else's recipe. I have tried throughout this book to mention swap options to address allergies, but keep these general tips in mind if you need to make adjustments for your family:

- **Use any dairy-free version of milk or cheese that I call for.** (You may need to try a few different brands to find one you prefer. There is a giant range when it comes to how well different brands of nondairy shredded cheeses melt, for example.)

- **Many people like using nutritional yeast in place of Parmesan cheese.** Start with less than the recipe calls for, then taste it and add more as you like.

- **For any recipe that uses wheat flour, sub in a cup-for-cup gluten-free flour blend.** (But straight almond or coconut flour is almost never a good direct substitute for wheat flour. You may still be able to make it work, but the results are almost guaranteed to be different from the original recipe.)

- **For any recipe that uses shellfish, sub in another fish of choice.** Or try chicken tenders and adjust the cooking time as needed.

- **In many cases, you can omit sausage and make the recipe vegetarian or sub in your favorite kind of beans.**

- **You can substitute any type of rice that I mention for one you have or prefer.** Just look at the instructions on your package to make sure you cook it properly.

- **Use your preferred type of tortilla**, though keep in mind that ones labeled "soft" (flour or ones that are a flour–corn blend) typically roll or fold more easily than ones made with corn only or without grains.

Farro–White Bean Salad Bowl,
page 102

A Final Note on Portion Size

A serving size is listed for each recipe. Most of the time, these recipes can feed four to six people, with a few that are suitable for up to eight diners. But keep in mind that those are very, very general estimations of portion sizes and hunger, and your unique family may need more or less food for a meal.

There is nothing wrong if your family of four needs more food.

And it is not a problem if your family needs less food.

Many recipes include portion sizes that are dictated by "diet culture." Diet culture is the system of beliefs that appearance and body size are more important than physical, emotional, or general well-being; the belief that controlling the amount and types of food you eat is more important than having access to food, being comfortable around a range of foods, or awareness of how food makes you feel. Taking portion sizes out of that context is difficult, but what really matters is how much food you and your family need to feel satisfied at any given meal. So it's important to me that we're all on the same page about the purpose of serving sizes. In the context of this book, they are simply to help you estimate which other foods you may or may not need to add to the meal to ensure that it's satisfying for your family. They're *not* provided to tell you (or you kids) how much to eat.

I know there may be questions, and that it's harder to comment and ask questions here than it is in the digital realm where I spend most of my time. But if you do ever have a question or you want to chat about food or you want to share how you made a recipe work for your family, please know that you can always reach me through the contact page on yummytoddlerfood.com or on social media @yummytoddlerfood.

Enjoy!
Amy

PASTA

It's probably no surprise that we always have pasta in the pantry—it's the one staple that my kids always like, plus it's so versatile and quick to cook. And while they might prefer to have their pasta plain with butter, I've found that there are recipes that I can make to gently expand their preferences. For example, we enjoy our favorite Italian-style pastas but also incorporate rice noodles, ramen noodles, and more into our meal plans. I've found that this allows us to explore a variety of flavors because there's always a familiar one (the pasta or noodles) as the base ingredient.

The types and shapes of pasta and noodles available in any one grocery store may vary widely, so see which options you have and go from there. Use whichever type of pasta you prefer, whether that's traditional semolina pasta or other options made from whole-wheat flour, lentils, chickpeas, or another ingredient. Just be sure to adjust the cooking instructions as directed on the package.

And know that most of these recipes have pieces of veggies and meat that are large enough to easily eat around if needed. This allows maximum flexibility for recipes and kids (or adults!) who may not love every component of the dish, but may be happy to eat some of them.

LEMON-BROCCOLI ORZO

Using some of the cooking water from the pasta to make a quick sauce with the lemon and Parmesan ensures this dish is brightly flavored, moist, and rich—the starch from the pasta is helpful that way! And the pasta water helps keep the ingredient list streamlined in this satisfying vegetarian meal.

SERVES: 8

PREP TIME: 10 minutes

COOK TIME: 10 minutes

TOTAL TIME: 20 minutes

1 pound orzo pasta

4 cups broccoli florets

¼ cup unsalted butter

½ cup grated Parmesan cheese, plus more for serving (optional)

Juice from ½ lemon, plus 1 tablespoon finely grated lemon zest

Fine sea salt and black pepper

1. Bring a large pot of salted water to a boil over high heat. Add the pasta and cook according to the package directions, setting a timer for the lower end of the cooking time *minus* 4 minutes. (So, if it says the pasta cooks in 10 to 12 minutes, set the timer for 6 minutes.)

2. When the timer goes off, add the broccoli to the pot with the pasta.

3. Reserve ½ cup cooking water. (I ladle it out into a small measuring cup or bowl.)

4. Drain the pasta and broccoli, transfer to a large bowl, and add the butter, Parmesan, lemon juice, lemon zest, and reserved cooking water.

5. Season the pasta with salt and pepper.

6. Serve the pasta with additional Parmesan, if desired.

NOTES

- If the flavor of lemon is new to the kids, cut back to 1 tablespoon of the lemon juice. If everyone loves it, feel free to add the second tablespoon.

- Use any pasta you like in this recipe. We prefer smaller shapes such as orzo, wagon wheels, or mini shells, but really, any type can work. Just be sure to adjust the cooking time according to the package directions.

- Adults may like this topped with crushed red pepper.

To make the recipe gluten-free: Swap in a favorite brand of gluten-free pasta.

To cut down on cost a little: Use grated Pecorino Romano in place of the Parmesan.

Pick a protein: Add a can of drained and rinsed white cannellini beans or 8 ounces cooked shrimp or diced rotisserie chicken, which may make it a little more filling.

SWEET POTATO MAC & CHEESE

Mixing sweet potato into mac and cheese adds flavor, nutrition, and creaminess—and it's also just really delicious. Use a store-bought sweet potato puree (though look for baby food that's mainly sweet potato, not a sweet potato blend with a lot of fruit). Or roast a sweet potato at home (recipe follows) and mash it with a fork or puree in a blender. This works with butternut squash puree too!

SERVES: 8

PREP TIME: 5 minutes

COOK TIME: 15 minutes

TOTAL TIME: 20 minutes

1 pound small pasta
(such as mini gears, stars, elbows, or shells)

2 tablespoons
unsalted butter

½ cup sweet potato puree

1½ cups shredded
cheddar cheese

½ cup milk

Fine sea salt and
black pepper

1. Bring a large pot of salted water to a boil over high heat. Add the pasta and cook according to the package directions.

2. Drain the pasta and return to the pot.

3. Stir the butter, sweet potato puree, cheese, and milk into the pasta and season with salt and pepper.

4. Serve the pasta warm.

NOTES

- Add a pinch of crushed rosemary for additional flavor.

- Sub shredded Monterey Jack cheese, fontina, or an Italian blend cheese, if preferred.

- Sprinkle leftover mac and cheese with water before reheating to help ensure it's as creamy as it was when you first made it.

ROASTED SWEET POTATO PUREE

MAKES: ½ CUP

1 medium sweet potato

1. Preheat the oven to 400°F.

2. Using a knife, poke a few holes in the potato. Place in a pie plate or on a baking sheet and bake for about 1 hour, or until very soft.

3. Discard the peel and, using a fork, mash the potato until very smooth (or blend in a blender) before using.

Add a veggie: In Step 2, drain the pasta over 2 cups frozen peas. Continue with the recipe.

PESTO PASTA, TWO WAYS

Pesto is so versatile. You can mix it with pasta and serve it warm or let it cool and mix in a few other ingredients to turn it into a satisfying pasta salad. Any store-bought pesto will work here, though you can make your own if you prefer. I love to keep pesto in the freezer if I have leftovers. For tips on freezing and thawing pesto, see page 29.

SERVES: 6 TO 8

PREP TIME: 10 minutes

COOK TIME: 10 minutes

REST TIME: 15 minutes

TOTAL TIME: 35 minutes

PESTO PASTA SALAD

1 pound pasta (such as orecchiette, elbows, spaghetti, or farfalle)

½ cup pesto (see page 47)

1 medium cucumber, diced

1 cup halved cherry tomatoes

One 14-5-ounce can white cannellini beans (drained and rinsed) or 2 cups thawed frozen peas

Fine sea salt

1. Bring a medium pot of salted water to a boil over high heat. Add the pasta and cook according to the package directions.

2. Drain the pasta and transfer to a large bowl.

3. Stir the pesto into the pasta and let cool for about 15 minutes. Then stir in the cucumber, tomatoes, and beans. Season with salt.

4. Serve the pasta at room temperature.

NOTES

- Use a 10-ounce package of refrigerated tortellini instead of dried pasta, if you prefer. If making that substitution, decrease the amount of pesto to ⅓ cup.

- I like English cucumbers since they tend to have smaller seeds and thinner skin—which I leave on—for a more pleasant chewing experience when eating the pasta salad.

- Vary the pasta type according to what you and your family like best. (Short shapes, like elbows, farfalle, or orecchiette, are often easier to eat in a pasta salad since they're a similar size to the rest of the ingredients.)

recipe continues

WARM PESTO PASTA

1 pound pasta (such as orecchiette, elbows, spaghetti, or farfalle)

½ cup pesto (recipe follows)

1 cup cooked diced chicken (optional)

1 cup halved cherry tomatoes (optional)

Grated Parmesan cheese for serving (optional)

1. Bring a medium pot of salted water to a boil over high heat. Add the pasta and cook according to the package directions.

2. Drain the pasta and return to the pot.

3. Stir the pesto into the pot and mix in the chicken and tomatoes (if using).

4. Serve the pasta topped with Parmesan cheese, if desired.

HOMEMADE PESTO

MAKES: ABOUT 1 CUP

1 cup lightly packed basil leaves

1 cup lightly packed parsley leaves

¼ to ½ cup olive oil

¼ cup grated Parmesan cheese

¼ cup roasted sunflower seeds

Fine sea salt

In a blender or food processor combine the basil, parsley, ¼ cup of the olive oil, Parmesan, and sunflower seeds. Blend until smooth, adding the remaining ¼ cup olive oil as needed to make a velvety mixture. Season with salt. Transfer to an airtight freezer bag and store in the freezer for up to 6 months.

NOTES

• Use baby spinach in place of the herbs for a more mellow-flavored pesto.

• Add 2 tablespoons fresh lemon juice to brighten the flavor.

CAPRESE SPAGHETTI

SERVES: 8

PREP TIME: 5 minutes

COOK TIME: 10 minutes

REST TIME: 5 minutes

TOTAL TIME: 20 minutes

4 medium tomatoes, diced

⅓ cup olive oil

¼ cup shredded basil

½ teaspoon fine sea salt

1 pound pasta (such as angel hair or spaghetti)

8 ounces pearl-style mozzarella balls, drained

Cracked black pepper

This pasta hits the spot any time of the year, but particularly in the summer when fresh tomatoes and basil are in season and abundant. It has such great fresh flavor and it's crazy fast. We usually have it with a side of Italian bread or rotisserie chicken—though it's delicious on its own too . . . even if the kids decide to ignore the tomato and eat just the noodles.

1. Place the diced tomatoes in a large bowl. Add the olive oil, basil, and salt and toss gently. Set aside to marinate while you cook the pasta.

2. Bring a large pot of salted water to a boil over high heat. Add the pasta and cook according to the package directions.

3. Drain the pasta and add to the bowl with the tomato mixture. Let sit for 5 minutes to cool just slightly.

4. Add the mozzarella to the bowl and toss to combine.

5. Serve the pasta topped with cracked black pepper, if desired.

NOTES

- If you can't find the tiny "pearl" mozzarella balls, you can dice up an 8-ounce ball of fresh mozzarella.

- I like using angel hair spaghetti here since it cooks so fast, but use another kind if you prefer.

- Use kitchen scissors to quickly cut up the cheese and the pasta for kids.

- Heirloom tomatoes are particularly flavorful, so use those if you have access to them. (If not, just be sure to choose a tomato that's fully ripe.) Cherry tomatoes work too.

To add flavor: In Step 1, add 2 garlic cloves, peeled and smashed, to the bowl. Discard the garlic before adding the pasta. (It's really spicy raw!)

Pick a protein: Add cooked diced chicken or shrimp, white beans, or chickpeas to make it more filling.

ONE-POT PASTA PRIMAVERA

PREP TIME: 10 minutes

COOK TIME: 20 minutes

TOTAL TIME: 30 minutes

1 pound fettuccini or linguini

1 pound frozen veggie medley (green beans, carrots, corn, and peas)

1 medium zucchini, ends discarded and thinly sliced (about ¼ inch thick)

2 tablespoons unsalted butter

½ cup heavy cream

½ cup reduced-sodium chicken stock or vegetable stock

½ cup grated Parmesan cheese, plus more for serving (optional)

½ teaspoon fine sea salt

Lemon wedges, cracked black pepper, and/or crushed red pepper for topping (optional)

With the classic flavors of pasta primavera but a simpler cooking method, this is a favorite weeknight meal that could also be fancy enough to share with company. The adults in my family like this with an additional squeeze of lemon and crushed red pepper on top, while the kids prefer it plainer. I love using frozen veggies plus one fresh zucchini since it cuts way down on the prep time while still adding a variety of colors and flavors.

1. Bring a large pot of salted water to a boil over high heat. Add the pasta and cook according to the package directions, setting a timer for the lower end of the cooking time *minus* 4 minutes. (So, if it says the pasta cooks in 10 to 12 minutes, set the timer for 6 minutes.)

2. Add the frozen veggies and zucchini to the pasta and stir. Set the timer for 4 minutes more.

3. Drain the pasta and vegetables and return them to the pot.

4. Add the butter, cream, chicken stock, Parmesan, and salt to the pot and toss to gently combine with the pasta.

5. Serve the pasta with your choice of toppings, cutting up the noodles for younger kids as needed.

To make this dairy-free: Omit the butter and cream. Toss with 2 tablespoons olive oil and dairy-free Parmesan or nutritional yeast.

Pick a protein: Add 2 cups cooked, diced chicken.

SHORTCUT BOLOGNESE

PREP TIME: 10 minutes

COOK TIME: 20 minutes

TOTAL TIME: 30 minutes

1 pound fettuccini or preferred type of pasta

2 tablespoons olive oil

1 cup fresh or frozen mirepoix, or ⅓ cup each diced onion, carrot, and celery

1 pound ground beef

½ teaspoon fine sea salt

One 28-ounce jar marinara sauce

¼ cup heavy cream

¼ cup grated Parmesan cheese

Cracked black pepper (optional)

Flavor, texture, and a seriously easy method transform a handful of ingredients into epic Bolognese . . . that doesn't need hours and hours on the stove. The sauce cooks while the water for the pasta comes to a boil, so this is a 30-minute dinner that's a real reward at the end of a long day. (I've made this on vacation in rental houses a handful of times, and it's always amazing how few ingredients you need to make a really delicious meal.)

1. Bring a large pot of salted water to a boil over high heat. Add the pasta and cook according to the package directions.

2. Meanwhile, set a large skillet over medium heat and warm the olive oil. Add the mirepoix and stir to coat. Add the beef and sprinkle with the salt. Using a wooden spoon, break up the meat into smaller pieces. Cook for 8 to 10 minutes, or until the beef is mostly cooked through.

3. Add the marinara sauce to the beef, stir, and cover. Turn the heat to low, cover, and let simmer for 10 minutes, or until the pasta is finished cooking.

4. Drain the pasta, add to the meat sauce, and toss to coat. Stir in the cream and Parmesan.

5. Serve the pasta, warm, topped with pepper, if desired.

NOTES

- Double the sauce recipe and stash half in the freezer for future use.

- Use half beef and half pork or Italian sausage for more flavor in the meat sauce.

- Look for prechopped mirepoix, (a mix of minced carrot, celery, and onion), near the precut veggies in your produce aisle or frozen in the freezer aisle. You can also chop a celery rib, small carrot, and small onion to make the mixture.

To make this dairy-free:
Omit the cream and cheese.

SAUSAGE & BUTTERNUT SQUASH PASTA

The slightly sweet flavor of butternut squash works so well with Italian sausage and pasta that you really don't need to add much else to make a satisfying meal. The only potential prep necessary for this recipe involves cutting the squash if you start with a whole one, but use precut to save some work. You can also chop the squash up to 3 days ahead and store it in an airtight container in the fridge until you're ready to use it.

PREP TIME: 10 minutes

COOK TIME: 20 minutes

TOTAL TIME: 30 minutes

1 pound pasta (such as orecchiette, elbows, or farfalle)

1 tablespoon olive oil

1 medium butternut squash, peeled, chopped, and seeded, or 4 cups diced precut butternut squash

12 ounces cooked mild Italian sausage, cut into ½-inch-thick rounds

2 tablespoons unsalted butter

¼ cup grated Parmesan cheese, plus more for serving (optional)

Fine sea salt and black pepper

1. Bring a large pot of salted water to a boil. Add the pasta and cook according to the package directions.

2. Drain the pasta.

3. Meanwhile, in a large skillet over medium heat, warm the olive oil. Add the butternut squash and sausage and stir to coat. Cover and cook, stirring occasionally, for 15 to 18 minutes, or until the squash is just soft when poked with a fork.

4. Transfer the drained pasta to the skillet and stir in the butter and Parmesan. Season with salt and pepper.

5. Serve the pasta with additional Parmesan, if desired.

NOTES

- Look for precut butternut squash in the produce or freezer aisles.

- Uncooked Italian sausage, bulk or in casings, can work here, too, if that's what you have. The cooking time will be about the same, though you'll want to stir a few times during Step 3.

- If leftovers seem a little dry when reheating, sprinkle with a small amount of water or stock to put some moisture back into the mix.

To make this dairy-free: Omit the butter and cheese.

Add some greens: In Step 4, add a few handfuls of baby spinach to the skillet to wilt.

VEGGIE LO MEIN

SERVES: 6 TO 8

PREP TIME: 10 minutes

COOK TIME: 20 minutes

TOTAL TIME: 30 minutes

12 to 16 ounces Chinese-style lo mein or ramen noodles

3 tablespoons toasted sesame oil

2 cups very thinly sliced bell pepper (any color) cored and seeded; sliced mushrooms; and/or snow peas

2 cups shredded cabbage

½ cup reduced-sodium soy sauce

¼ cup honey or maple syrup

1 tablespoon freshly grated ginger, or 1 teaspoon ground ginger

Sriracha, halved or chopped peanuts, and/or lime wedges for topping (optional)

We used to live in a small town with limited takeout options, so I learned to make a few favorites at home. For this recipe, you can use lo mein noodles, "Chinese noodles," or spaghetti, so see what you can find. These noodle varieties come in packages ranging from 10 to 16 ounces, so make the full recipe for the sauce and add a little at a time to your liking. (I find that the noodles really absorb it, so we always use all the sauce.) You can prep the veggies while the pasta comes to a boil—or skip that step and use precut veggies from the store.

1. Bring a large pot of water to a boil over high heat. Add the noodles and cook according to the package directions.

2. Meanwhile, add 1 tablespoon of the sesame oil to a large skillet. Add the bell pepper and toss to coat. Cook for 8 to 10 minutes, stirring occasionally, or until the bell pepper is soft. Stir in the cabbage.

3. In a small bowl, stir together the soy sauce, honey, remaining 2 tablespoons sesame oil, and ginger to form a sauce.

4. Drain the noodles and add to the skillet with the veggies. Stir in the sauce.

5. Serve the lo mein with your choice of toppings.

NOTES

- Look for shredded cabbage in a bag. It's often near the coleslaw in the produce aisle. Use up any leftover cabbage instead of lettuce in tacos or on a sandwich.

- If this is a new style of noodles for the kids, offer a small pair of kids' scissors so they can chop up the noodles on their own. This can help them engage with the food in a pressure-free way.

- Avoid honey for kids under the age of one year.

Pick a protein: Add 2 cups chopped fully cooked chicken or shrimp or frozen (thawed) shelled edamame.

RED CURRY RICE NOODLES WITH CARROTS & TOFU

SERVES: 6 TO 8

PREP TIME: 15 minutes

COOK TIME: 10 minutes

TOTAL TIME: 25 minutes

1 pound extra-firm tofu

14 ounces stir fry–style rice noodles

2 tablespoons toasted sesame oil

5 ounces shredded carrots

1 cup canned light coconut milk

¾ cup Homemade Thai-Style Red Curry Sauce (facing page)

Fresh lime slices, hot sauce, sliced green onions (green part only), peanuts, and/ or cilantro for topping (optional)

I like using rice noodles in this dish since they pair so well with Thai-style curry. (They're also a convenient allergy-friendly option to wheat-based noodles for gluten-free families.) Look for Thai-style red curry sauce near the soy sauce in your store. I add coconut milk as I find it helps make the bottled curry sauce taste more like what you'd get at a restaurant.

1. Drain the tofu and press firmly with a clean kitchen towel to absorb the water.

2. Dice the tofu into approximately 1-inch cubes.

3. Prepare the noodles according to the package directions. (Rice noodles usually need to be rinsed to remove extra starch—don't skip that step if your package calls for it as it helps keep them from sticking or clumping together.) Drain.

4. Meanwhile, in a medium nonstick or cast-iron skillet over medium heat, warm the sesame oil. Add the tofu and cook for 5 minutes.

5. Flip the tofu, add the carrots, and cover. Cook for 5 to 7 minutes more, or until the tofu is slightly golden brown and the carrots are just softened.

6. Add the noodles to the skillet. Add the coconut milk and curry sauce and toss gently with a pair of kitchen tongs or a big fork.

7. Serve the noodles with your choice of toppings.

NOTES

- Feel free to swap in a store-bought teriyaki or peanut sauce for the red curry to vary the flavor of the dish.

- Use chicken instead of tofu, or spaghetti instead of rice noodles.

- Use the leftover coconut milk in a smoothie or in place of regular milk in oatmeal. Or freeze it in an ice-cube tray to use when you make this recipe again.

HOMEMADE THAI-STYLE RED CURRY SAUCE
MAKES: ABOUT 2 CUPS

One 14.5-ounce can light coconut milk
2 tablespoons red curry paste
1 tablespoon brown sugar
1 tablespoon reduced-sodium soy sauce
2 teaspoons lime juice

In a large bowl, stir together the coconut milk, curry paste, brown sugar, soy sauce, and lime juice. Store in the fridge in an airtight container for up to 2 weeks or in a freezer bag in the freezer for up to 6 months.

GINGER CHICKEN RAMEN NOODLES

This quick ramen is endlessly customizable—and builds on pantry basics of stock and noodles. In my house, we like this with chicken and broccoli but see the Notes for other ideas. Look for packages of slightly wavy ramen noodles (which are sometimes called "Chinese noodles"). The sizes of the package may vary based on the brand you find, so increase the stock a little if your package is larger than the 10-ounce package that I call for.

SERVES: 4 TO 6

PREP TIME: 5 minutes

COOK TIME: 15 minutes

TOTAL TIME: 20 minutes

10 ounces ramen noodles

One 32-ounce carton reduced-sodium chicken stock

2 tablespoons grated ginger

2 tablespoons reduced-sodium soy sauce

1 pound chicken tenders or chicken breast

4 cups broccoli florets

Toasted sesame oil, chopped peanuts, lime juice, and/or hot sauce for topping (optional)

1. Bring a large pot of salted water to a boil over high heat. Add the noodles and cook according to the package directions.

2. Drain the noodles and return to the pot.

3. Meanwhile, in a medium pot over high heat, warm the chicken stock. When it starts to boil, turn the heat to medium and bring to a simmer.

4. Add the ginger and soy sauce to the stock. Using kitchen scissors, cut small pieces of the chicken directly into the stock. (This saves you from dirtying a cutting board.) Let simmer for 4 minutes.

5. Stir the broccoli into the pot and continue to cook for another 4 minutes, or until the broccoli is just tender when poked with a fork.

6. Add the noodles to the pot with the stock mixture and toss to coat.

7. Serve the ramen with your choice of toppings.

NOTES

- Use cauliflower, shredded carrots, or peas in place of the broccoli.

- Cut up the noodles with kitchen scissors for little kids. (They can use kid-safe kitchen scissors to do it themselves too.)

- The stock flavor is key here, so try a few brands to see what you like best. Or add some chicken bouillon to amp up the flavor.

- For tips on freezing and grating fresh ginger, see page 29.

Pick a protein: Instead of chicken, swap in diced extra-firm tofu, shrimp, edamame, or thinly sliced steak.

QUICK TORTELLINI & PEA SOUP

Simmering store-bought tortellini in chicken or vegetable stock is such a simple way to cook this pasta. This soup is comforting and filling with a hit of frozen peas that are stirred in right at the end. Top this with grated Parmesan or Pecorino Romano cheese, or stir in a spoonful of pesto or a squeeze of lemon juice. Serve with crackers or toast, if desired.

SERVES: 4 TO 6

PREP TIME: 5 minutes

COOK TIME: 10 minutes

TOTAL TIME: 15 minutes

1 quart reduced-sodium chicken stock

1 pound fresh cheese tortellini

2 cups frozen peas

Fine sea salt

Grated Parmesan cheese, pesto, crushed red pepper, and/or lemon juice for topping (optional)

1. In a medium saucepan over medium-high heat bring the chicken stock to a simmer.

2. Add the tortellini to the stock and cook for 8 to 10 minutes, or as directed on the package, until tender.

3. Remove the pan from the heat and stir in the peas. Season with salt.

4. Serve the soup, warm, with your choice of toppings.

NOTE

• Use a 5-ounce bag of baby spinach in place of the peas. Stir in to wilt the spinach.

Pick a protein: Add frozen meatballs to add a new flavor to this soup. You may need to add more stock with this option.

THE
MAGIC
OF A
MEAL
ROTATION

I can hardly remember life before my husband and I had kids, but I do know that dinner was much easier to sort out simply because there was less going on at the end of the day. As our family grew, we had to change the way we thought about dinner to save our sanity.

Enter: A Meal Rotation

I started looking around at the people in my life who seemed to be able to pull off making a variety of meals on a regular basis, including everyone who had a lot of kids in the mix, and I realized that our daycare was a perfect model. They put together a basic menu for the month, but during that month there were both small changes (like apples and crackers for snack one day and pears and crackers for snack the next) *and* many of the foods appeared multiple times. This allowed the kids to become familiar with foods over time—and took some of the decision-making off the table for the food director.

I think many of us feel as though we need to make new recipes constantly, but I have learned that having a regular cast of favorites that we cycle through makes everything easier. And it can help the kids be a little more willing to consider new foods because they always know they'll see their favorites again soon. I adapted the basic method from our first daycare for our family and now do a monthly meal rotation that's built around the idea of themes. Each night of the week has a basic dinnertime category such as tacos, pasta, soup or salad (depending on the time of year), pizza, takeout, and so on. The categories can be whatever you want them to be, but the beautiful part is that if you decide on them ahead of time, you're never starting from scratch when planning dinner.

"Tacos" is a much easier place to start than just staring into the fridge because, with a category, you have parameters. But within that category, you also have flexibility. This means you can use what you have on hand, adjust if an activity runs late or you run out of an ingredient, and generally always feel like you have at least some semblance of a plan. And it's also easier to keep pantry staples on hand when you know what these regular categories are for your family. (For me, this means I always have beans, tortillas, pasta, and jarred sauce in the pantry!)

It is reassuring for kids to know that they will see foods they love on a regular basis. And, over time, it can help kids learn to like (or at least be willing to consider one day) foods when they see the rest of their family enjoying them a few times a month. Two of my kids learned to love black beans this way—over the span of about two years, which, yes, is a lot of time. But it was a totally low-pressure way to continually expose the kids to foods we hoped they would one day eat. And now they do.

You can write out a plan for the whole month, do it week by week, or pick even three nights a week with a theme. You can do the same system each week or alternate. It's totally flexible so you can really make it work for your family and your context. Anything that helps us make fewer decisions come mealtime is a win to me.

Here's an example of what a dinner rotation might look like for a week in my house.

SUNDAY: **Soup**

MONDAY: **Pasta**

TUESDAY: **Tacos**

WEDNESDAY: **Skillet Meal**

THURSDAY: **Sandwiches**

FRIDAY: **Takeout**

SATURDAY: **Salad**

—OR—

SUNDAY: **Slow-Cooker Meal**

MONDAY: **Soup and Salad**

TUESDAY: **Meal in a Bowl**

WEDNESDAY: **Takeout**

THURSDAY: **Grilled Meat**

FRIDAY: **Pizza**

SATURDAY: **Kids' Choice**

SANDWICHES & SALADS

There is often so much pressure on us to make "real" dinners and to save such options as sandwiches and salads for lunch . . . or to wait to serve big salads until the kids are much older. But—and this is a really important "but"—you can throw that silly advice right out the window! Both sandwiches and salads are great options to have in the mix, especially since they are so easy to customize for all ages. And you can either just assemble them or quickly cook them and serve them up to share.

Sandwiches can be deconstructed for toddlers for easier eating. Use all sorts of breads—sliced sandwich bread, pita, naan, flatbread, rustic bakery-fresh bread, or another option you love. They can be open-faced toast-type offerings or fillings stuffed into rolls or pita bread. And salads can be based on lettuce, sure, but also built on noodles—with lots of veggies in the mix.

All of which is to say, we can break the "rules" and use whatever food idea for whichever meal we like if it works for our family; sandwiches and salads included. Here you'll find choices for both categories, with a lot of no-cook options in the mix for those nights when even turning on the stove is just too much. Use whichever variations you need, and enjoy those quick meals . . . whenever you need them.

VEGGIE HUMMUS FLATBREAD

This sandwich is a satisfying weeknight dinner—whether you wrap the fillings up gyro-style or serve it like a flatbread pizza. You can adjust this however you like—add sliced red onions, leftover chicken, use another cheese . . . so many options. For this recipe, you can use pita bread, lavash, naan, or any whole-grain flatbread you prefer. Many kids love assembling these by themselves.

SERVES: 4 TO 6

PREP TIME: 10 minutes

COOK TIME: 0 minutes

TOTAL TIME: 10 minutes

6 multigrain flatbreads

One 10-ounce container hummus

2 cups shredded lettuce

1 medium cucumber, thinly sliced

1 medium tomato, sliced

½ cup crumbled feta or goat cheese

½ cup sliced Greek olives

Oregano for sprinkling

Lemon wedges for squeezing (optional)

1. Working with one flatbread at a time, toast lightly in a toaster or warm on a heat-safe plate in the microwave for about 15 seconds.

2. Spread the flatbread with a layer of hummus and add any of the toppings that you or the kids like.

3. Sprinkle with oregano and a squeeze of lemon juice, if desired.

4. Fold up the flatbread into a sandwich or serve open-faced like a pizza and eat with fingers or a fork and a knife.

NOTES

- We enjoy this meal with a side of fruit (like grapes) or soup.

- Replace pita pockets with another type of flatbread or a wrap that you like.

- Use whichever flavor of hummus your family prefers. (I'm partial to classic.)

- I like to look in the bakery section of my grocery store to see what types of flatbread are freshly baked (though almost any option is delicious if slightly warmed and topped with goodness).

Pick a protein: Add cooked and diced chicken, shrimp, or chickpeas to the flatbread.

OPEN-FACED BROCCOLI MELTS

I am always shocked at how much my kids love these veggie toasts—which are such an easy (and unexpected) dinner. We sometimes even have them as an appetizer when we have soup for dinner (and using the word *appetizer* can instantly make it seem special to kids). Serve with rotisserie chicken, scrambled eggs, or cut-up fruit as desired.

SERVES: 4 TO 6

PREP TIME: 5 minutes

COOK TIME: 8 minutes

TOTAL TIME: 13 minutes

12 ounces frozen broccoli florets

One 12-ounce loaf multigrain bread, Italian bread, or sourdough bread, cut into 1-inch slices

¼ cup unsalted butter

1 tablespoon finely grated lemon zest, plus 1 tablespoon lemon juice

6 slices mozzarella cheese

1. Prepare the broccoli according to the package directions.

2. Drain the broccoli in a colander and pat dry with a clean kitchen towel.

3. Using kitchen scissors, coarsely mince the broccoli.

4. Meanwhile, turn the broiler to high and place the bread on a baking sheet. Lightly toast for 2 minutes. Remove from the oven.

5. Spread the bread with the butter and then cover with the broccoli. Add a little lemon zest and lemon juice to each slice. Top with a half slice of mozzarella—or as much as you need to cover the top of each slice of bread.

6. Put back under the broiler for 2 minutes, or until the cheese melts and is just starting to brown.

7. Serve the toasts warm.

NOTES

• Use fresh broccoli if you prefer. Place fresh broccoli into a pot and just cover with water. Bring to a boil over medium-high heat and cook for 4 to 6 minutes, or until fork-tender.

• Swap in cauliflower, peas, or halved cherry tomatoes for the broccoli to vary this meal.

• Sprinkle the toasts with a little salt before serving, if desired.

• Store leftovers in the fridge in an airtight container for up to 5 days. Reheat on a baking sheet in a 375°F oven for 4 to 6 minutes, or in a toaster oven until warmed through.

Pick a protein: Add white beans or thawed frozen peas to the toast to make it a little more filling.

PIZZA BREAD

PREP TIME: 5 minutes

COOK TIME: 10 minutes

TOTAL TIME: 15 minutes

1 French bread loaf or baguette

½ cup pizza sauce

1 cup toppings (such as pepperoni, sliced olives, minced cooked broccoli, very thinly sliced raw mushrooms, or cooked Italian sausage; optional)

2 cups shredded mozzarella cheese

¼ cup grated Parmesan cheese

1 teaspoon pizza seasoning

Grab a loaf of French bread, or a baguette, and a jar of pizza sauce and you're just minutes away from dinner. This is nice for when you want to mix up your usual pizza routine or if you have fresh bread to use up. We like this with thinly sliced mushrooms, sliced black olives, and, sometimes, pepperoni, but you can add any toppings you choose. You can also make this in a toaster oven, if you prefer. Pair with a simple salad (such as BLT Caesar Salad, page 82) or another favorite side dish to round out this meal.

1. Preheat the oven to 400°F.

2. Cut the bread in half, horizontally, and then each half in half, widthwise, to make four pieces. Place them on a baking sheet.

3. Evenly divide the pizza sauce on the bread, spreading it to the edges. Add your choice of toppings. Top with the mozzarella, Parmesan, and pizza seasoning.

4. Bake the pizzas for 8 to 10 minutes, or until the cheese is just starting to brown. Remove from the oven and let cool for a minute or two.

5. Using a serrated knife or kitchen scissors, cut the pizzas into individual pieces to serve.

NOTES

• For a burst of freshness, sprinkle with minced parsley after pulling from the oven.

• Use gluten-free bread and nondairy cheese as needed.

• Let the kids add their own mix of toppings to personalize this meal . . . if you have the energy to have more cooks in the kitchen!

SLOPPY JOE SANDWICH POCKETS

The day that I figured out how to stuff loose-meat sandwich filling into a roll—rather than slicing the roll and having all the meat mixture fall out when the kids went to eat it—was a happy one. This pocket sandwich requires only a few pantry staples. I love to use soft brioche-style rolls in this since they are so fluffy and tender, but any unsliced roll will work. Pair with french fries or Roasted Potatoes (page 244) and maybe some fresh fruit to round out the meal.

SERVES: 4 TO 6

PREP TIME: 5 minutes

COOK TIME: 10 minutes

TOTAL TIME: 15 minutes

1 tablespoon unsalted butter or olive oil

1 pound ground beef or ground turkey

2 tablespoons ketchup

1 tablespoon tomato paste

½ teaspoon oregano

½ teaspoon fine sea salt

6 unsliced rolls

1. Set a medium nonstick or cast-iron skillet over medium heat. Add the butter and swirl to melt.

2. Add the beef to the skillet and, using a wooden spoon, break it up into smaller pieces. Continue cooking for 8 to 10 minutes more, or until the meat is cooked through and no longer pink. (If there's a lot of liquid or fat in the pan, you can drain it off.) Add the ketchup, tomato paste, oregano, and salt and stir.

3. Meanwhile, using a small knife, make a slit on one side of each roll. Using your fingers, open the slit to make a pocket in the roll where the filling can go. (Try not to cut all the way through.)

4. Fill each pocket to the brim with the meat, pressing it in gently.

5. Serve the sandwich pockets warm.

NOTES

- These sandwiches are great with simple sides, including pickles, sliced melon, corn on the cob, or roasted potatoes.

- If you prefer your Sloppy Joes saucier, add another 2 tablespoons ketchup.

- Use mini slider rolls to make these smaller for little kids.

Add a veggie: In Step 2, add 1 cup finely minced green bell pepper and ½ cup minced onion to cook with the beef.

PEPPERS & EGG SANDWICHES

SERVES: 6 TO 8

PREP TIME: 5 minutes

COOK TIME: 15 minutes

TOTAL TIME: 20 minutes

2 tablespoons unsalted butter or olive oil

2 medium bell peppers (any color), cored, seeded, and diced

½ teaspoon fine sea salt

½ teaspoon onion powder

8 eggs

½ cup shredded mozzarella or cheddar cheese

6 to 8 ciabatta rolls, sliced and warmed or toasted

Hot sauce for drizzling (optional)

While this classic Italian American sandwich of eggs, bell peppers, onions, and cheese was a staple at our local pizza place back when I was a kid, I now rely on it as a super-fast dinner option for weeknights with my family. I modify it a little by cooking the peppers and eggs side by side in the pan—to give more options for serving this to family members who may not like their foods all mixed together—but the flavors are still similar. Ciabatta rolls are a delicious choice for this sandwich.

1. Set a large nonstick skillet over medium heat. Add the butter and swirl to melt.

2. Add the bell peppers, salt, and onion powder to the skillet and stir to coat. Cover and cook for 8 to 10 minutes, or until the bell peppers are just soft when poked with a fork. Push them to one side of the skillet. Turn the heat to medium-low.

3. Crack the eggs into the other side of the skillet. (Yes, really—you don't have to whisk them in a separate bowl.) Using a spatula, gently break the yolks and then cook, stirring occasionally to allow the raw egg to flow under the cooked egg. Cook until the eggs are set, about 5 minutes.

4. Stir the cheese into the eggs and then turn off the heat.

5. Serve the peppers and eggs on the rolls or side by side on a plate with hot sauce for drizzling, if desired.

NOTES

- Set aside a few slices of raw bell pepper before you start cooking. These are for the kids who prefer their peppers crisp and crunchy.

- Use toasted sliced Italian bread instead of rolls.

- Mix the peppers and eggs all together rather than keeping them separate.

- For variety, use broccoli florets instead of the bell peppers.

CRISPY
FISH
SANDWICHES

Disclaimer: This recipe requires your hands to be messy for a bit, so set the kids up with an activity (or a podcast or a screen!) for 5 to 10 minutes so you can get it into the oven. Then? Enjoy perfectly flaky and crispy fish that's ready to pair with rolls and simple toppings. Add some sliced apples or a simple salad on the side to round it out.

SERVES: 6

PREP TIME: 10 minutes

COOK TIME: 10 minutes

TOTAL TIME: 20 minutes

¼ cup all-purpose flour

2 eggs, lightly beaten

1 cup panko or Italian-seasoned bread crumbs

1 pound tilapia fillets (fresh or frozen and thawed according to the package directions)

½ teaspoon fine sea salt

6 sliced rolls

Lettuce, mayo, tartar sauce, ketchup, lemon juice, and pickles for topping (optional)

1. Preheat the oven to 425°F. Line a rimmed baking sheet with aluminum foil and coat lightly with nonstick spray. Set aside.

2. Place the flour, eggs, and panko into separate wide bowls in a little assembly line.

3. Add each piece of fish to the flour, then the eggs, and then the panko, coating them completely.

4. Set the fish on the prepared baking sheet. Sprinkle with the salt.

5. Bake the fish until lightly golden brown and cooked through, about 10 minutes.

6. Divide the fish among the rolls and serve with your choice of toppings.

NOTES

- This fish is best on the day it's made, but you can heat leftovers on a baking sheet in a 375°F oven for 4 to 6 minutes, or until warmed through. Try not to heat longer than that to avoid drying out the fish.

- Use mayo instead of the beaten eggs.

- Use chicken tenders instead of fish and increase the cooking time to 14 to 16 minutes.

- Serve the sandwich elements side by side to make chewing easier for younger eaters.

Make it gluten-free: Use a 1:1 gluten-free flour for the all-purpose flour.

Make it faster: Use frozen prepared fish sticks or breaded fish fillets from the freezer aisle in your store. Cook according to the package directions.

RICE NOODLE SALAD WITH PEANUT SAUCE

Noodle-based salads are great starter salads to share with the kids (since noodles or pasta is often inherently more appealing than lettuce). This one has both noodles and veggies for a refreshing mix with a lot of texture. I like to use stir fry–style rice noodles in this salad, though any rice noodle will work. Be sure to rinse them under cold water after cooking to help prevent them from sticking together.

SERVES: 6 TO 8

PREP TIME: 5 minutes

COOK TIME: 8 minutes

TOTAL TIME: 13 minutes

14 ounces stir fry–style rice noodles

1 medium cucumber

1 cup coleslaw mix

½ cup chopped roasted and salted peanuts, plus more for serving (optional)

½ cup bottled peanut sauce

Fresh cilantro, fresh mint, edamame beans, drained extra-firm tofu, and cooked shrimp for serving (optional)

1. Prepare the noodles according to the package directions. Drain in a colander and rinse with cold water.

2. Cut the cucumber into thin "matchsticks," discarding the ends.

3. Transfer the noodles to a large bowl and add the cucumber, coleslaw, peanuts, and peanut sauce. Toss to mix everything together.

4. Serve the salad with your choice of toppings.

NOTES

- Dress any leftover coleslaw mix with the remaining peanut sauce to make an easy lunch salad.

- Use thin vermicelli or cellophane rice noodles (or even angel hair pasta), if you prefer.

- I prefer English cucumbers to other types since their skin is thinner and more tender and their seeds tend to be smaller. This means you don't have to peel them to make them pleasant to eat. Or you can use a few mini cucumbers.

- Chop the peanuts more finely for kids under age 2.

For a nut-free version: Use teriyaki sauce and sesame seeds instead of peanut sauce and peanuts.

Pick a protein: Include baked tofu, chicken tenders (see page 238), scrambled eggs, or edamame beans in this dish to make it more filling. (Look in the frozen vegetable section of your food store to find edamame beans without the pods; prepare according to the package directions.)

BLT CAESAR SALAD

SERVES: 4 TO 6

PREP TIME: 10 minutes

COOK TIME: 15 minutes

TOTAL TIME: 25 minutes

8 slices bacon

Family-size bagged Caesar salad kit (16 to 17 ounces) or two smaller bags

2 medium tomatoes, diced

1 to 2 medium avocados, skinned, pitted, and sliced

6 ounces cooked chicken breast

Pick a protein: Try canned white cannellini beans (drained and rinsed) in place of the chicken.

Make it faster: Skip the bacon completely or use bacon crumbles that you can buy from the supermarket.

Real talk: Caesar salad kits have been the gateway salad in our house. They were the first way that my kids learned they liked lettuce, and it has been so amazing to have it as a fast dinner option. Sure, the three of them do argue over who has the most croutons, but I still love how much they enjoy the crunchy, crisp goodness. And when you pair it with bacon, chopped tomato, avocado, and some cooked chicken? Well, that right there is a dinner win.

1. Preheat the oven to 400°F. Line a rimmed baking sheet with aluminum foil and line a plate with a layer of paper towels.

2. Arrange the bacon in a single layer on the prepared baking sheet and bake until cooked to your preferred level of crispiness, about 15 minutes. Using a fork or tongs, carefully transfer the bacon to the prepared plate. Pat to dry.

3. In a large bowl, combine the salad, tomatoes, and avocado. Cut the chicken into small pieces, crumble the bacon, and then add them to the salad. (I like to add the toppings in little groupings so it's easier to give everyone just the ones they want—then I can mix it together on my own plate.)

4. Serve the salad immediately.

NOTES

- Use 1 pint of cherry tomatoes instead of chopping full-size tomatoes. Halve them vertically for kids under age 4.

- Add a side of bread or toast, if desired.

- Vary this recipe by starting with any salad kit you prefer, or make your own with a base of lettuce and croutons and a dressing of choice.

- If buying the components of Caesar salad—romaine lettuce, shredded Parmesan cheese, croutons, and dressing—and assembling it yourself is less expensive than prepackaged, you can always go that route too.

AVOCADO CHICKEN SALAD

Rotisserie chicken is so versatile, and it forms a flavorful base in this chopped chicken salad. It's delicious stuffed into a pita as a sandwich or served platter-style so everyone can choose the elements they prefer and eat it with a fork (or, in the case of little kids, their hands). We like this with a side of fruit or chips.

SERVES: 4

PREP TIME: 10 minutes

COOK TIME: 0 minutes

TOTAL TIME: 10 minutes

2 cups chopped rotisserie chicken or other cooked chicken

2 medium avocados, pitted and diced

One 14.5-ounce can fire-roasted corn, drained and rinsed

¼ cup minced cilantro

2 tablespoons olive oil

1 tablespoon lime juice

¼ teaspoon fine sea salt

4 whole-grain pita rounds

1. In a medium bowl or on a platter, compose the chicken, avocados, corn, and cilantro. Drizzle the olive oil and lime juice on top and sprinkle with the salt.

2. Leave deconstructed or toss together according to your preference.

3. Cut each pita round in half and fill with the salad. Or you can simply cut the pita into wedges and serve as a side with the salad.

NOTES

- Add more lime or some minced jalapeños, as desired. You can also add a little minced red onion to your serving.

- Pick up pita chips instead of pita bread and use the salad as a dip.

- Use a 14.5-ounce can chickpeas in place of the chicken to make this vegetarian. Drain, rinse, and pat the beans dry before adding them to the bowl. You may need to add a little salt.

- If you can't find fire-roasted corn, use sweet corn—canned or thawed from frozen. Or use fresh sweet corn, cooked until tender and cut off the cob.

- Add quartered grapes or diced pear to bring a little sweetness to this salad.

ULTIMATE FAMILY CHARCUTERIE BOARD

SERVES: 4 TO 6

PREP TIME: 10 minutes

COOK TIME: 0 minutes

TOTAL TIME: 10 minutes

1 to 2 cups protein: shredded cheese, canned beans (drained and rinsed), shredded cooked chicken, cooked shrimp, hard-cooked eggs

1 to 2 cups veggies: thinly sliced bell pepper, cucumber, or carrot; snap peas; halved cherry tomatoes

1 to 2 cups fruit: halved or quartered grapes, berries, sliced melon, clementine segments, thinly sliced apple or pear, canned fruit, raisins

2 to 4 cups carbohydrates: crackers, sliced bread, diced muffin, pita chips

½ to 1 cup dips or sauces: hummus, guacamole, ranch dressing, salsa, cucumber sauce, or any other dip your family enjoys

A giant charcuterie plate is a perfect way to use up a variety of foods you may have lingering in the fridge—and can be a festive, yet easy way to end the day. You can serve everything on a platter or assemble individual plates of food. We love this as a picnic dinner during warm weather, so, often, I intentionally buy a few special cheeses, meats, spreads, and crackers. Or we just forage in the fridge and pantry and make little groupings of miscellaneous foods. You can build around a theme (such as "cheese plate," "hummus platter," and so on) or keep it really random.

Arrange your chosen ingredients on a platter to serve family-style so everyone can help themselves. Or put some of the foods on each person's plate.

NOTES

- Let the kids choose options to add to the mix to help them buy into the meal before they even get to the table.

- Pick at least one option from the listed food groups at left. Add as many more as you want.

- Thinly slice raw veggies lengthwise to ensure they are easier for toddlers to chew.

- Vertically halve or quarter grapes and cherry tomatoes for kids younger than 4 years.

Make it faster: Start with a veggie or fruit plate from the supermarket to skip right over the chopping! Add some cheese and bread to round it out.

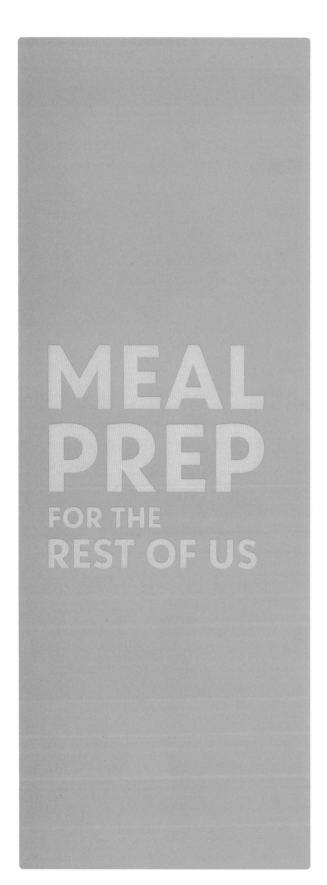

MEAL PREP
FOR THE REST OF US

Scroll through any social media feed, especially on the weekend, and you'll see videos and images of beautiful containers of fully prepped food. (Often, the food is arranged to make rainbows.) And while I fully understand how spending a few hours to make food on the weekend can save time during the rest of the week, most parents I know simply don't have the schedule—or energy—for that style of cooking. Or they feel guilty if they sometimes do it and sometimes don't, or if they only do a little prep and not a countertop full.

If meal prep works for you and brings you joy, embrace it. If you want to be a little more prepared without that level of time commitment, keep reading. Since planning ahead can help when those busy weeknights strike, here's the happy medium I've found . . . which doesn't take over the entire weekend (because we deserve to rest and relax, too, which is already hard enough for most of us!).

Prep One Veggie Side Dish Ahead

I often peel and chop a bunch of carrots or broccoli florets after I get home from the grocery store and keep them in an airtight container. Then, when I'm in the middle of making dinner on a busy weeknight, I can simply dump the container into a skillet or roasting pan to cook. Just doing one meal's worth helps yet isn't overwhelming to pull off.

Rely on Prepared Veggies

Salad kits, washed lettuces and veggies, precut fruit . . . yes, they sometimes cost a little more, but if it means you are actually able to serve rather than skip the produce, this can be a great option to have in the mix. Compare prices at different stores where you shop since some store brands offer considerably lower prices than name brands.

Stock the Freezer with Frozen Veggies

The single best way I know to minimize food waste and simplify cooking veggies is to use more frozen ones. This means that I can buy less fresh produce and have less pressure to use it before it goes bad. I simply keep a stash of quick-cooking frozen veggies on hand. They often cook faster than fresh and require zero chopping. (Frozen vegetables and fruits are frozen right after picking, which seals in the nutrients and freshness. Which is a great thing. Thank you, food science.)

And there are many fresh vegetables that you can freeze if you won't have a chance to use them before they spoil. I love to freeze raw fresh spinach, kale, cauliflower, and zucchini to add to future soups. Those are good to throw into smoothies too.

Cook Twice as Many Grains

Whenever I'm making rice, quinoa, or farro, I cook twice as much as I need for one meal and stash half in the freezer for a future week. (Or in the fridge to use as leftovers for lunches.) Cooked grains freeze so well and can be thawed at room temperature during the day while you're doing life. Sprinkle the grains with a little water before reheating to help them fluff back up to their just-cooked consistency. (Cooking twice as much also works for homemade pizza sauce and most sauces, homemade pizza dough, chicken tenders, breads, muffins, oatmeal, and more.)

Prep Two Snacks at Once

This is such a simple idea but one that helps me offer my kids the fruit they love when they ask for it. I cut up two snacks' worth of strawberries, mango, pineapple, cucumbers, or carrots at once. This helps us use what we buy, and having that stash of prepped produce on hand (in portioned snack containers) makes things so much easier on subsequent days since the fruit is ready to grab and serve.

Double Favorite Recipes

If I'm making a recipe that I know my family loves, I often make twice as much so we have it for lunch (or dinner) the following day. There's no shame in eating the same foods more often if it simplifies life!

BOWLS

The concept of a "bowl"—which is, quite literally, a mix of foods served in a bowl—is a simple way to assemble meals with a variety of flavors and textures. And they're inherently so versatile. This style of recipe is also particularly straightforward to serve deconstructed—for younger eaters who may not love their food all mixed together—since you can simply plate the ingredients side by side. It allows so much flexibility, which can increase the odds of pleasing a variety of preferences or food intolerances in one fell swoop. Consider this your invitation to play with the suggested ingredients and let everyone mix and match as they like. There's no one right way to make these recipes.

Also, remember that you can change up the base of these bowls as you like. While I may call for rice or pasta or another grain, you can simply swap it out for an option that you prefer or happen to have on hand. I know that might feel intimidating, but any should work fine, so switch and swap as you like.

P.S. Most of these are great as leftovers for lunch the following day, too, so enjoy!

SHRIMP FAJITA BOWLS

SERVES: 4 TO 6

PREP TIME: 10 minutes

COOK TIME: 20 minutes

TOTAL TIME: 30 minutes

1 cup uncooked jasmine rice, basmati rice, or other preferred rice

1 tablespoon vegetable oil or unsalted butter

2 medium bell peppers (any color) stemmed, seeded, and thinly sliced

1 small white or yellow onion, thinly sliced

1 pound uncooked shrimp (fresh or frozen), peeled and deveined

1 teaspoon cumin

½ teaspoon chili powder

½ teaspoon fine sea salt

Salsa, guacamole, sour cream, and fresh lime for topping (optional)

Relying on quick-cooking shrimp and store-bought condiments allows you to re-create the yummy flavors of takeout fajita bowls at home with less work. Want to save even more prep time? Use precut frozen bell peppers instead of starting with fresh. (If starting with frozen shrimp, thaw according to the package directions first—which may mean putting it into the fridge on the morning of the day you plan to make this or running under cold water.) These bowls are great with rice and topped with sour cream and guacamole. Remember that it's okay if the kids don't want every element of this meal—or any meal. Add a simple side of applesauce or shredded cheese, if needed, to make sure they have one or two foods on the table they usually like. This ensures that there's plenty to fill their tummies.

1. Cook the rice according to the package directions, or until it is soft and most of the liquid has been absorbed. Turn off the heat, cover, and set aside.

2. In a large skillet over medium heat, warm the vegetable oil. Add the bell peppers and onion, stir to coat, and then cook for 8 minutes, stirring once or twice.

3. Add the shrimp, cumin, chili powder, and salt to the vegetables and stir to coat. Cook for 3 to 4 minutes and then flip the shrimp. Cook for 2 to 3 minutes more, or until the shrimp are opaque and cooked through.

4. Serve the fajita mixture over the rice with your choice of toppings.

NOTES

- Save a step by choosing shrimp that's already peeled and deveined.

- Use a 16-ounce bag of frozen sliced peppers instead of fresh if you'd like to skip the chopping.

- Use fully cooked rice from the store—for options, look in both the freezer aisle and near the dried grains and beans.

- Replace the spices in the recipe with 1 to 2 teaspoons taco seasoning, if that's easier.

CHEESE-BURGER BOWLS

These bowls offer the flavor of cheeseburgers with more veggies and without the fuss of having to form ground beef into patties. (It's also a great option to share with younger kids who may not quite be able to bite into the thick stack of a regular burger just yet.) Add whichever condiments the kids like, try a salad dressing, or try my family's Burger Bowl Sauce.

SERVES: 4 TO 6

PREP TIME: 10 minutes

COOK TIME: 10 minutes

TOTAL TIME: 20 minutes

1 tablespoon olive oil or unsalted butter

1 pound ground beef

½ teaspoon garlic powder

½ teaspoon onion powder

½ teaspoon oregano

½ teaspoon fine sea salt

4 cups chopped romaine lettuce

1 cup shredded cheddar cheese

Tomatoes, red onion, pickles for topping (optional)

Burger Bowl Sauce (recipe follows) for serving

Rolls for serving (optional)

1. In a large skillet over medium heat, warm the olive oil. Add the beef and, using a wooden spoon, break it up into small pieces. Stir in the garlic powder, onion powder, oregano, and salt and cook, stirring occasionally, for 8 to 10 minutes, or until the meat is evenly cooked through and browned. Drain off any excess liquid.

2. Divide the lettuce among individual bowls. Add the meat mixture, cheese, and your choice of toppings.

3. Serve with bowl sauce, as well as rolls, if desired.

NOTES

- Store any leftover beef in an airtight container in the fridge for up to 5 days. Warm briefly to serve.

- Use ground turkey, ground chicken, or cooked lentils in place of the beef.

- Increase or decrease your choice of toppings.

- Swap in roasted potatoes or French fries for the rolls—or serve in addition to them.

- If the kids do want to eat this as a sandwich, simply add the cooked meat to the roll as you would a Sloppy Joe. (See page 74 for how to make this style of sandwich less messy.)

BURGER BOWL SAUCE
MAKES: ½ CUP

¼ cup ketchup

¼ cup mayonnaise

1 tablespoon pickle juice (Yes, from a jar of pickles!)

In a medium bowl, stir together the ketchup, mayonnaise, and pickle juice. This sauce is a great option for drizzling on classic burger flavor.

Coconut Rice Bowls
with Mango, page 98

COCONUT RICE BOWLS WITH MANGO

A little sweet, a little savory—this grain bowl has flavor and nutrients and is still quick to accomplish at the end of the day. I love making sure that each spoonful has a few bits of each ingredient (it's so, so good that way—must have a bite of mango in each spoonful!). My kids often eat as much mango as possible first and then try the rest. Whatever works! Photograph on pages 96–97

Photograph on pages 96–97

SERVES: 4 TO 6

PREP TIME: 15 minutes

COOK TIME: 15 minutes

TOTAL TIME: 30 minutes

1 tablespoon coconut oil (refined or unrefined)

1-inch piece fresh ginger

3 cups water

One 14.5-ounce can coconut milk

1½ cups uncooked jasmine rice

2 cups frozen shelled edamame

1 tablespoon maple syrup or honey

½ teaspoon fine sea salt

2 large mangoes, diced

Minced red onion and cilantro for topping (optional)

1 lime, cut into wedges (optional)

1. In a large saucepan over medium heat, melt the coconut oil.

2. Using a Microplane, grate the ginger into the oil and stir to coat. Cook for 1 minute.

3. Add the water and coconut milk to the pan, turn the heat to high, and bring to a boil.

4. Add the rice to the pan, turn the heat to medium, and let simmer for 12 to 15 minutes, stirring occasionally, or until the rice is soft and the liquid is mostly absorbed.

5. Stir the edamame, maple syrup, and salt into the rice. Turn off the heat, cover, and let sit for 5 minutes.

6. Transfer the mixture to a serving bowl and top with the mango and your choice of other toppings.

7. Serve the grain bowl with a squeeze of lime juice (or not!).

NOTES

- You can thaw 2 cups of frozen diced mango to skip cutting up fresh ones. And at certain times of the year, when available, the smaller and more yellow-skinned variety of Ataulfo mangoes are often less expensive than other kinds and seriously delicious.

- Add some cooked cocktail shrimp to the top of each bowl if more protein is desired.

- In Step 4, add 2 tablespoons shredded unsweetened coconut to the pot with the rice for more coconut flavor.

- Replace the edamame beans with black beans.

- For tips on freezing and grating fresh ginger, see page 29.

- Wrap fresh herbs in a paper towel and store in a plastic bag in the fridge to help them last long enough for you to use them up. The paper towel helps absorb excess moisture.

VEGGIE BURRITO BOWLS BAR

SERVES: 4 TO 6

PREP TIME: 15 minutes

COOK TIME: 25 minutes

TOTAL TIME: 40 minutes

2 medium sweet potatoes, peeled and diced

2 tablespoons olive oil

¼ teaspoon fine sea salt

1½ cups uncooked short-grain brown rice

One 14.5-ounce can black beans, drained and rinsed

2 cups shredded lettuce

2 cups shredded cheddar cheese

Salsa, diced avocado, guacamole, cilantro, and sour cream for topping (optional)

Letting the family make their own burrito bowls can please everyone at the table—even if no two people have identical plates. You can cook the sweet potatoes and rice up to 3 days ahead and stash them in the fridge if you might be short on time when you plan to serve this. Then, set out the ingredients and let everyone assemble their own bowl (or, in the case of little kids, ask them which foods they'd like to have their bowl). Photograph on page 100

1. Preheat the oven to 425°F.

2. On a rimmed baking sheet, toss the sweet potatoes with the olive oil and salt. Roast for 20 to 25 minutes, or until soft.

3. Meanwhile, in a medium saucepan, cook the rice according to the package directions, or until the rice is soft and most of the liquid has been absorbed. Turn off the heat and cover.

4. Place the beans into a microwave-safe bowl and microwave for 1 to 2 minutes, or until warmed through.

5. Serve the potatoes, rice, and beans with the lettuce, cheese, and your choice of other toppings.

NOTES

• Take a shortcut and simmer frozen diced sweet potatoes in water until tender. Or swap out the potatoes completely and use frozen corn. In Step 4, warm the corn with the beans.

• Warm up fully cooked rice from the store to save one step of cooking.

• Using a big platter to serve the foods can help cut down on how many dishes you use.

Veggie Burrito Bowls Bar,
page 99

FARRO–WHITE BEAN SALAD BOWLS

Roasted sweet potatoes are one of those simple ingredients that adds so much flavor to this grain bowl—especially when mixed with other veggies. Farro is a slightly chewy, nutty grain that cooks quickly and stores well in the fridge or freezer once cooked. You can prepare the sweet potatoes and farro up to five days ahead of making this meal. Stash them in airtight containers in the fridge until you're ready to assemble. Serve this mixed together or put it in separate bowls and let everyone decide which ingredients to add to their plates. Photograph on page 36

SERVES: 4

PREP TIME: 10 minutes

COOK TIME: 20 minutes

TOTAL TIME: 30 minutes

2 medium sweet potatoes, peeled and diced

2 tablespoons olive oil

¼ teaspoon fine sea salt

2 cups cooked farro (see facing page)

One 14.5-ounce can white cannellini beans, drained and rinsed

5 ounces baby spinach

¼ to ½ cup bottled green goddess dressing

1 cup grated or diced sharp cheddar cheese

1 medium apple, thinly sliced

Croutons, roasted sesame seeds, and/or dried cherries for topping (optional)

1. Preheat the oven to 425°F. Line a rimmed baking sheet with aluminum foil or parchment paper.

2. Place the sweet potatoes on the prepared baking sheet, toss with the olive oil, and sprinkle with the salt.

3. Bake the potatoes until just soft, about 20 minutes. Remove from the oven and let cool slightly.

4. In a large bowl, combine the farro, beans, spinach, and sweet potato. Pour in the dressing, starting with the ¼ cup and adding more as you like, then add the cheese, apple, and your choice of toppings.

5. Toss well and serve. (You can also serve this family style and let everyone choose the ingredients and toppings they prefer.)

NOTES

- Use cooked pasta or brown rice in place of the farro.
- Use a different dressing if there's one that your family prefers.
- Omit the farro to cut down on cooking and serve with a side of whole-grain bread.
- Simmer frozen diced sweet potatoes to avoid peeling and dicing fresh ones.

Pick a protein: Add diced cooked chicken or shrimp.

SOFT & TENDER FARRO
MAKES: ABOUT 2 CUPS

1 cup farro
4 cups water
Fine sea salt

1. Place the farro in a fine-mesh sieve and rinse with cold water. (Sometimes there is a dusty coating on the grains.)

2. Transfer the farro to a large pot and add the water and a pinch of salt. Set over high heat, bring to a boil, and then turn the heat to medium-low and let simmer for 25 to 30 minutes, or until the farro is just tender. (It should be chewy, but not hard.) Drain and let cool.

3. Store the farro in an airtight container in the fridge for up to 5 days, or in the freezer for up to 3 months.

MEDITER-RANEAN HUMMUS BOWLS

A few basic spices and a container of hummus can lend a lot of flavor to plain ingredients—and mix up how you usually serve rice and beef. You could add a side of pita bread or pita chips to this as an option for dipping into the hummus. (That usually makes my kids very happy.) The mix of textures here, with the crunchy, crisp cucumbers and salty olives over the base of softer ingredients, makes the experience of eating the bowl really pleasant.

SERVES: 4 TO 6

PREP TIME: 10 minutes

COOK TIME: 10 minutes

TOTAL TIME: 20 minutes

1 tablespoon olive oil

1 pound ground beef or ground turkey

1 small red onion, peeled and thinly sliced

½ teaspoon oregano

½ teaspoon cumin

¼ teaspoon garlic powder

¼ teaspoon fine sea salt

1 cup uncooked rice or other grain (such as quinoa, couscous, or farro)

½ cup hummus

Juice from ½ lemon

2 tablespoons water

1 pint cherry tomatoes, halved lengthwise

1 medium cucumber, cut into rounds

1 cup black olives or olive of choice, drained

½ cup crumbled goat cheese or feta cheese

6 cups pita chips (see page 107; optional)

1. In a medium skillet over medium heat, warm the olive oil. Add the beef, onion, oregano, cumin, garlic powder, and salt and, using a wooden spoon, break up the meat and cook for 8 to 10 minutes, or until it is fully browned. (If there's a lot of liquid or fat in the pan, drain it off.)

2. Meanwhile, cook the rice according to the package directions, or until it is soft and most of the liquid has been absorbed. Turn off the heat and cover.

3. In a medium bowl, combine the hummus, lemon juice, and water. Stir to make a thick dressing.

4. Place some of the rice in each serving bowl. (I usually give about 1 cup for adults and ½ cup for kids, but adjust as you like.) Top with some of the beef mixture, hummus dressing, tomatoes, cucumber, olives, cheese, and pita chips—customizing to serve every plate as each person prefers.

NOTES

- You can make the rice up to 5 days ahead. Let it cool slightly and then store in an airtight container in the fridge. Sprinkle the rice with a little water before reheating. Or buy fully cooked rice from the store.

- Omit the onion and olives, if you want. Or add a sprinkle of freshly chopped parsley.

- Use flavored hummus (such as roasted red pepper) to vary the flavors.

Pick a protein: Replace the ground beef with chickpeas, hard-cooked eggs, or white beans to make this meat-free.

GREEK SALAD BOWLS

Combining flavorful store-bought foods in these bowls is a fast way to offer a delicious meal. This recipe is both easy and seriously delicious. Any kind of precooked chicken will work—even two chicken breasts from the grocery store's prepared foods case, leftover chicken, rotisserie chicken, or chicken nuggets. If you don't feel like toasting pita rounds, use a 12-ounce bag of pita chips.

SERVES: 4

PREP TIME: 10 minutes

COOK TIME: 0 minutes

TOTAL TIME: 10 minutes

1 medium cucumber, cut into rounds or sticks

1 sweet bell pepper (any color), cut into strips

1 pint cherry tomatoes, halved

1 pound cooked chicken breast, diced into bite-size pieces

12 ounces hummus

4 ounces diced cheddar cheese or crumbled feta cheese

1 batch Homemade Pita Chips (recipe follows)

12 ounces tzatziki sauce

Arrange the cucumber, bell pepper, tomatoes, chicken, hummus, cheese, and pita chips on a big serving platter so everyone can help themselves. Put tzatziki on the side to pass around so people can drizzle into their bowls.

NOTES

- Serve this over a bed of chopped romaine lettuce, if you prefer.

- Look for tzatziki near the hummus or in the prepared-foods aisle of your store. If it's not an ingredient you have access to, simply skip it.

- Add a drizzle of a favorite vinaigrette—Greek dressing or Caesar dressing is yummy here too—and add cracked black pepper on top for more flavor.

HOMEMADE PITA CHIPS
MAKES: 6 TO 8 CUPS

6 whole-wheat pita rounds

Olive oil for brushing

Fine sea salt

1. Preheat the oven to 400°F.

2. Using kitchen scissors, cut the pita rounds into triangles. Arrange them on two baking sheets, brush with olive oil (a pastry brush works great), and sprinkle with salt.

3. Bake the triangles for 8 to 10 minutes, or until lightly browned. (These are less crunchy, usually, than store-bought ones and may be easier for kids under age 3 to chew.)

4. These are best on the day they are made but leftovers can be stored in an airtight container at room temperature for up to 3 days.

Pick a protein: Replace the chicken with cooked sliced steak, sautéed tofu, chickpeas, or hard-cooked eggs.

CHOPPED-SALAD PASTA BOWLS

Turn a big chopped salad into family dinner by adding pasta (or another preferred grain) and a protein. I love how easy this meal is to deconstruct for the kids—for example, those who prefer pasta to be separate from their cucumbers can have them next to each other on their plate—or to enjoy mixed together as an adult. You can also play around with the proportion of lettuce to pasta if you or your family prefer more of one than the other.

SERVES: 4

PREP TIME: 10 minutes

COOK TIME: 10 minutes

REST TIME: 10 minutes

TOTAL TIME: 30 minutes

8 ounces pasta (such as orecchiette, elbows, or farfalle)

1 tablespoon olive oil

One 5-ounce bag chopped romaine lettuce

1 medium cucumber, chopped

1 pint cherry tomatoes, halved lengthwise

One 14.5-ounce can chickpeas or other bean, drained and rinsed

1 cup croutons

¼ cup shaved Parmesan cheese

¼ to ½ cup Italian dressing

Pick a protein: Instead of the beans, use pan-seared tofu or any cooked chicken or shrimp.

1. Bring a large pot of water to a boil over high heat. Add the pasta and cook according to the package directions. Drain the pasta, toss with the olive oil, and let cool slightly for 5 to 10 minutes.

2. Meanwhile, in a big bowl, combine the lettuce, cucumber, and tomatoes. Top with the pasta, chickpeas, croutons, and Parmesan.

3. If serving family-style and everyone is deciding what to put into their bowl, offer the dressing to each person to drizzle on or use as a dip. Or, if making one big salad, start with about ¼ cup of dressing and toss to coat. Add the remaining ¼ cup dressing as desired.

NOTES

- You can make the pasta ahead of time, if desired. After completing Step 1, simply store in an airtight container in the fridge. When you are ready to use it, let sit at room temperature for about 30 minutes before mixing with the rest of the ingredients. Or if it's straight out of the fridge, heat in the microwave for a minute to soften.

- Add chopped hard-cooked eggs and crumbled cooked bacon for more flavor.

- Swap in 2 cups cooked brown rice, farro (see page 103), or quinoa in place of the pasta.

- Use balsamic vinaigrette, ranch, or Caesar dressing, if you prefer.

- Cook a full pound of pasta, put half in the salad, and keep half on the side to toss with butter and Parmesan, which gives the kids another option.

UNSTUFFED PEPPER BOWLS

Take the flavors of stuffed peppers but skip the stuffing and baking steps and you have this favorite weeknight meal. This has been a staple in our house for almost a decade and is both comforting and so fast to make. You can start with fresh bell peppers and dice them, or use frozen precut peppers. Serve this flavorful mixture over any type of rice your family enjoys, or even with pasta.

SERVES: 4 TO 6

PREP TIME: 10 minutes

COOK TIME: 14 minutes

TOTAL TIME: 24 minutes

1½ cups rice (long- or short-grain, white or brown)

1 tablespoon unsalted butter or olive oil

1 pound ground turkey or ground beef

1 teaspoon garlic powder

1 teaspoon onion powder

1 teaspoon oregano

½ teaspoon fine sea salt

2 medium bell peppers (any color), cored, seeded, and diced

One 14.5-ounce can crushed tomatoes

1 cup shredded mozzarella cheese

Shredded basil leaves for topping (optional)

1. Cook the rice according to the package directions, or until it is soft and most of the liquid has been absorbed. Turn off the heat, cover, and set aside.

2. Meanwhile, in a large skillet over medium heat, melt the butter.

3. Add the turkey, garlic powder, onion power, oregano, and salt to the skillet and, using a wooden spoon to break up the meat, cook for 2 minutes.

4. Add the bell peppers and tomatoes to the skillet, cover, turn the heat to medium-low, and let simmer for 10 to 12 minutes, or until the peppers are soft. Remove the cover and stir.

5. Serve the mixture over the rice and top with the cheese and basil, if desired.

NOTES

- Add 2 garlic cloves, minced, for more flavor.
- Top your portion with crushed red pepper.
- Use diced tomatoes instead of crushed, if that's what you have.
- As a last step, while the food is still in the pan, sprinkle with the cheese and pop under the broiler to brown and melt.
- Use sausage rather than the turkey for extra flavor.

EGG ROLLS IN A BOWL

PREP TIME: 5 minutes

COOK TIME: 12 minutes

TOTAL TIME: 17 minutes

1½ cups uncooked rice (such as jasmine or basmati)

1 tablespoon coconut oil or vegetable oil

1 pound ground chicken

2 garlic cloves, peeled and minced, or 1 teaspoon jarred minced garlic

1 teaspoon minced ginger, or ½ teaspoon ground ginger

One 7- to 9-ounce bag finely shredded cabbage

2 to 3 tablespoons reduced-sodium soy sauce

1 tablespoon toasted sesame oil

1 teaspoon maple syrup

Sliced green onions (green part only) for topping (optional)

Wonton strips or crackers for topping (optional)

Make it vegetarian:
Substitute firm tofu, drained and crumbled, for the meat.

This bowl has all the flavor of egg rolls without the mess of frying or the need to wait for takeout. Yes! We like this bowl served over rice (which ensures that it's filling enough for my family), though you can skip the grain if you prefer. Look for wonton strips near the croutons in your grocery store. They add a nice crunch to this meal (and are delicious to eat on their own too!).

1. Cook the rice according to the package directions, or until it is soft and most of the liquid has been absorbed. Turn off the heat, cover, and set aside.

2. Meanwhile, in a large skillet over medium heat, melt the coconut oil. Add the chicken, garlic, and ginger and, using a wooden spoon to break up and stir the meat, cook for 8 to 10 minutes, or until the chicken is browned, cooked through, and no longer pink.

3. Add the cabbage, soy sauce, sesame oil, and maple syrup to the skillet, stir well, and cook for 4 minutes more, or until the cabbage is wilted and just tender.

4. Serve the mixture over the rice, topped with green onions and wonton strips, if desired.

NOTES

- Use ground pork or ground turkey instead of chicken. After Step 2, drain the fat from the pan if you see a lot of it. (You are more likely to need to do that if using pork.)

- Use half cabbage and half carrots to vary the flavor.

- If the kids aren't into cabbage, you can swap with another veggie, like peas or even broccoli.

- Try over ramen noodles if that's more appealing to your family.

- Cut the pieces of ingredients that the kids may not love—like green onions—large enough that you can easily take them out of their portion. That's much easier than trying to hide them in plain sight!

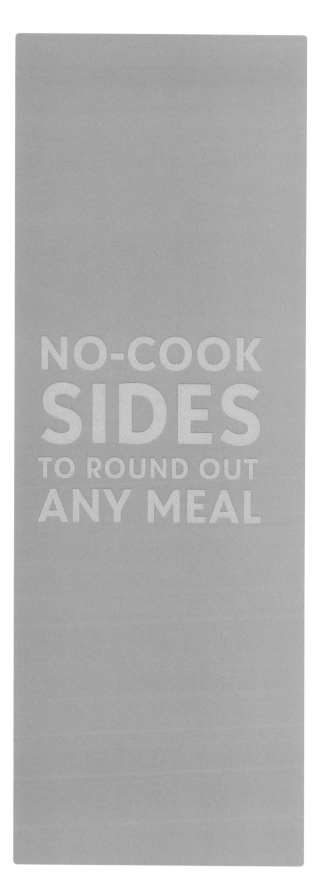

NO-COOK **SIDES** TO ROUND OUT ANY MEAL

This may sound really obvious, but you don't have to cook side dishes to serve with dinner. Fully believing that simple sentence can free you up to really streamline meals and incorporate delicious options that take much less work to make.

I love to rely on these no-cook sides to round out meals that I make for my family. They're also the easiest way I know to ensure that each meal I offer my family of five includes at least one food that each person usually likes. This helps me avoid short-order cooking for any one child, and it lets us all stay seated at the table for the duration of the meal. (Of course, there are still times we need to get up, but it's really minimized when I include one or two of these options!)

To minimize choking hazards, grate raw apples and carrots for kids younger than 12 months. Around 14 months, move to thin matchstick-size slices. After that, continue slicing raw produce thinly up until age 4—and avoid big chunks of hard produce, including apples and carrots—so kids can chew these foods more easily. And always cut round foods, such as grapes and cherry tomatoes, into vertical quarters or halves.

It helps to have low-cook cooking options too. Frozen French fries, frozen veggies, and take-and-bake breads are also yummy side dishes. So are canned veggies! Just warm them up according to the package directions and flavor as you like.

Here's my go-to list for no-cook sides for family meals. Add whichever ones you'd love to have in the mix:

Applesauce

Apples, sliced

Canned fruit in 100 percent juice

Canned veggies, drained and warmed

Carrots, sliced

Cheese

Crackers

Cucumbers, sliced

Frozen veggies, warmed

Italian bread

Naan bread

Oranges

Pears, sliced

Pita bread

Pita chips

Rotisserie chicken

Salad kits

Yogurt

SHEET-PAN MEALS

The concept of tossing a few foods together on a sheet pan is not new, but I hope these recipes remind you of how great an option this style of cooking can be for families (or any busy people!). The main goal with these oven meals is ease of both prep and cooking; you should be able to get the food into the oven and then walk away to do whatever else needs doing.

You may want to add sides to some of these meals to make them more substantial for your family, add more toppings to build in layers of flavor, or even change one of the veggies to please your people. These are great base recipes to start with and adjust as you like.

Unless otherwise indicated in the recipe, I'm using a standard half-sheet pan here—and it's rimmed, which helps keep the food from falling off the sides. If you have a smaller oven, you can use two quarter-sheet pans. If you want to double any recipe, just use two half-sheet pans and cook them at the same time on different racks in the oven. Depending on the style of your oven, you may want to rotate the two pans (swapping their positions as well as turning each one around) halfway through so the foods cook evenly.

And for faster cleanup, line your pan with aluminum foil or parchment paper, coating with nonstick spray if indicated in the recipe.

TILAPIA & VEGGIES WITH TOAST

I like to use tilapia for this meal since it's a thin fish and cooks quickly. It's also a relatively inexpensive option that's lower in mercury (fish high in mercury can be a concern for pregnant women and young children). The fish cooks to a perfectly tender texture while the spinach wilts and the tomatoes soften—all on the same pan. This meal is so good with a side of crusty bread.

SERVES: 4 TO 6

PREP TIME: 10 minutes

COOK TIME: 12 minutes

TOTAL TIME: 22 minutes

One 5-ounce bag baby spinach

1 pint cherry tomatoes

Four 6-ounce tilapia fillets

Juice from ½ lemon

2 tablespoons olive oil

½ teaspoon fine sea salt

¼ teaspoon oregano

4 slices whole-grain bread

2 tablespoons unsalted butter

1. Preheat the oven to 425°F. Line a half-sheet pan with parchment paper.

2. Layer the spinach and tomatoes on the prepared pan and top with the fish. Drizzle with the lemon juice and olive oil, and sprinkle with the salt and oregano.

3. Place the bread on a separate sheet pan.

4. Place the fish pan on the middle oven rack and the bread pan on the bottom oven rack. Bake for 10 to 12 minutes, or until the fish is opaque and flakes easily with a fork.

5. Meanwhile, spread the toasted bread slices with the butter.

6. Serve the fish with the buttered toast.

NOTES

- Adults may enjoy this topped with crushed red pepper.

- Set aside a few raw tomatoes for the kids if they prefer them that way. (Halve them lengthwise for kids under age 4.)

- Add a dip (such as ketchup or ranch or Caesar dressing) for the kids if they prefer to dip their food.

- Swap in salmon and increase the cooking time to 14 to 16 minutes to account for the increased thickness of that type of fish.

- To get a jumpstart on this, you can assemble the sheet pans through Step 3 in the morning, cover with plastic wrap, and refrigerate until dinnertime.

- Add more bread if you like.

BREAKFAST-FOR-DINNER FRITTATA

I am such a huge fan of eggs for dinner that we have them at least once a week in one form or another. They're packed with vegetarian protein and also (usually) inexpensive. This method of baking a frittata mixture over frozen hash browns is one of our favorites because it combines a few foods we love and, also, it's seriously satisfying. I make half with veggies and herbs and half plain so everyone is happy.

SERVES: 6 TO 8

PREP TIME: 10 minutes

COOK TIME: 30 minutes

TOTAL TIME: 40 minutes

One 10- to 12-ounce bag frozen hash browns

12 eggs

1 cup whole milk

½ teaspoon fine sea salt

1½ cups shredded cheddar cheese

1 cup cherry tomatoes, halved (optional)

2 tablespoons minced parsley (optional)

1. Preheat the oven to 375°F. Line a half-sheet pan with parchment paper and then coat the paper and the sides of the pan with nonstick spray to help prevent the frittata from sticking.

2. Spread the hash browns in one even layer across the pan and bake for 10 minutes.

3. Meanwhile, in a medium bowl, whisk the eggs, milk, and salt to combine well. Pour over the hash browns, spreading the mixture evenly. Sprinkle with the cheese and add the tomatoes and parsley (if using).

4. Bake the frittata for 18 to 20 minutes, or until firm to the touch and cooked through.

5. Slice the frittata and serve warm.

NOTES

- We usually have this with a simple salad and toast.

- Offer ketchup, salsa, or another favorite dip on the side so everyone has something they like.

- You can also serve this between two slices of buttered toast as a sandwich—we love to use up leftover frittata that way.

- Use nondairy milk and cheese as needed.

Pick a protein: Add black beans, diced cooked chicken, or cooked and crumbled bacon to this for more flavor.

SWEET POTATO NACHOS

PREP TIME: 10 minutes

COOK TIME: 24 minutes

TOTAL TIME: 34 minutes

2 pounds sweet potatoes
(such as garnet yams),
peeled and cut into ¼- to
½-inch-thick rounds

1 teaspoon ground cumin

½ teaspoon fine sea salt

Two 14.5-ounce cans black
beans, drained and rinsed

2 cups shredded
cheddar cheese

½ cup salsa

2 cups coarsely chopped
spinach

Thawed frozen corn, cooked
ground beef, and/or any
other toppings for serving
(optional)

Make it faster: Use frozen
sweet potato fries as the
base instead of starting with
fresh. Bake according to the
package directions, add your
choice of toppings, and warm
it through.

Using sweet potato as a base makes nachos easier for
younger eaters to chew (tortilla chips can be really difficult
for little kids) and, frankly, is just super-delicious. I like to
use part of the pan for toppings for the adults (like spinach
and sliced jalapeños) and another part for some for the
kids (like just corn)—so everyone has an area to dig into.
You can do this with regular potatoes, too, if that's what
you have or your family prefers. Use kitchen scissors to
quickly chop the spinach.

1. Preheat the oven to 400°F. Line a half-sheet pan with
parchment paper.

2. Place the potato rounds in an even layer on the prepared
pan. Sprinkle with the cumin and salt.

3. Bake the potatoes for 16 to 18 minutes, or until soft when
poked with a fork. Top with the beans, cheese, and salsa
and then bake for 4 to 6 minutes more, or until the cheese
is melted.

4. Serve the nachos, warm, with your choice of toppings.

NOTES

- You can assemble this recipe as directed in Step 3, then cover
and store in the fridge to bake later in the day if you want to
get ahead.

- Add a simple side of diced mango, pineapple, or any other fruit
the kids like.

ITALIAN SAUSAGE WITH BROCCOLI & POTATOES

Mild Italian sausage has so much flavor that you can toss it with basic veggies—like potatoes and broccoli—and have a tasty meal in no time. I use raw sausage links for this and cut them with kitchen scissors to make the prep quick. (No need to dirty a cutting board, simply cut them right into the sheet pan.) Purple- or red-skinned potatoes make this extra colorful, but any kind will work.

SERVES: 4 TO 6

PREP TIME: 5 minutes

COOK TIME: 28 minutes

TOTAL TIME: 33 minutes

1 pound mild uncooked Italian sausage links, cut into 1-inch rounds

4 cups or one 16-ounce bag broccoli florets

2 pounds baby potatoes, quartered

3 tablespoons olive oil

½ teaspoon fine sea salt

¼ teaspoon black pepper

Crumbled feta cheese for topping (optional)

1. Preheat the oven to 400°F. Line a half-sheet pan with parchment paper.

2. Place the sausage, broccoli, and potatoes on the prepared pan. Toss with the olive oil and sprinkle with the salt and pepper.

3. Bake the sausage and veggies for 24 to 28 minutes, or until the broccoli and potatoes are soft and the sausage is cooked through.

4. Serve the meal topped with feta, if desired.

NOTES

- Use pork, chicken, or turkey sausage, as you like.

- Add a pint of halved cherry tomatoes to the sheet pan in Step 2 for fresh flavor.

- To simplify the prep, I leave the peel on the potatoes. The skin on baby potatoes is usually very tender and pleasant to eat.

- Offer pesto, pizza sauce, ketchup, or another favorite dip alongside this.

FIFTEEN-MINUTE FLATBREAD PIZZA

There are so many delicious flatbreads available at the grocery store now, and they make perfect pizza crusts. That means you can have homemade pizza on the table in about 15 minutes. Look for flatbread in the bakery aisle of your grocery store to see what fresh options are available. Or use pita bread, lavash, or naan bread, which you can find in the bread aisle.

SERVES: 4

PREP TIME: 5 minutes

COOK TIME: 10 minutes

TOTAL TIME: 15 minutes

2 large flatbreads (8 to 10 inches in diameter or length)

½ cup pizza sauce

1 cup shredded mozzarella cheese

¼ cup grated Parmesan cheese

Sliced olives, cooked broccoli florets, sliced pepperoni, and other favorite pizza garnishes for topping (optional)

1. Preheat the oven to 425°F. Line a half-sheet pan with parchment paper or aluminum foil.

2. Place the flatbreads in the prepared pan and top with the pizza sauce, mozzarella, Parmesan, and your choice of garnishes.

3. Bake the pizza for 8 to 10 minutes, or until the cheese is melted and lightly browned. Remove from the oven and let cool for a minute or two.

4. Cut the pizza before serving.

NOTES

- Use Italian-blend shredded cheese or thinly sliced fresh mozzarella instead of the shredded mozzarella, if desired.

- Use a favorite nondairy cheese if needed.

- Add a salad kit, store-bought soup, or fruit on the side to round out this meal

- Dice flatbreads up for little kids or try serving in thin wedges.

GREEK CHICKEN BAKE WITH OLIVES

SERVES: 6 TO 8

PREP TIME: 5 minutes

COOK TIME: 30 minutes

TOTAL TIME: 35 minutes

One 25-ounce jar
  marinara sauce

1 pound boneless chicken
  breast or thighs

8 ounces button
  mushrooms, sliced

4 ounces pitted Greek olives

Crumbled feta cheese or
  goat cheese for topping

1 pound cooked pasta,
  2 cups cooked rice (see
  page 239), or 1 loaf Italian
  bread (optional)

Baking chicken in marinara sauce delivers consistently tender, moist meat in a totally hands-off way. Add olives, mushrooms, and a topping of goat or feta cheese for Greek flavors that pair well with pasta, rice, or bread. You can also make this in a glass baking dish or a 9 by 13-inch cake pan. In a pinch, a cast-iron skillet also works!

1. Preheat the oven to 375°F. Coat a half-sheet pan with nonstick spray.

2. Spread the marinara sauce in the bottom of the pan. Place the chicken on top of the sauce and the mushrooms on top of the chicken. Spoon up a little of the sauce so that it mostly covers everything. Evenly scatter the olives over the top.

3. Bake the chicken for 28 to 30 minutes, or until an instant-read thermometer registers 160°F.

4. Shred the chicken with two forks, top with the cheese, and serve with the pasta, rice, or bread, if desired.

NOTES

- Store leftovers in an airtight container in the fridge for up to 5 days.

- Use a 28-ounce can of tomato sauce in place of the marinara sauce, the latter often has more flavor but may also be more expensive. Use whichever you prefer.

Make it vegetarian: Omit the chicken and use two 14.5-ounce cans of chickpeas or white beans, drained and rinsed. Bake for 14 to 16 minutes, or until warmed through.

BAKED GNOCCHI WITH PEPPERS

Fresh gnocchi are so versatile and have a fun, fluffy-with-crispy-edges texture when baked on a sheet pan. (My kids call these "pasta pillows," which is a fairly accurate description.) You can use prepared pesto as a dipping sauce. Look for it near the hummus, Italian cheeses, or jarred pizza sauce in your store.

SERVES: 6 TO 8

PREP TIME: 10 minutes

COOK TIME: 16 minutes

TOTAL TIME: 26 minutes

1 pound fresh refrigerated gnocchi

1 pint cherry tomatoes

1 small red onion, peeled and thinly sliced

2 medium bell peppers (any color), cored, seeded, and thinly sliced

2 tablespoons olive oil

¼ teaspoon fine sea salt

¼ cup prepared pesto

Grated Parmesan cheese for topping (optional)

1. Preheat the oven to 450°F. Line a half-sheet pan with parchment paper.

2. Put the gnocchi, tomatoes, onion, and bell peppers in the prepared pan and toss with the olive oil and salt. Spread in an even layer.

3. Bake the gnocchi for 14 to 16 minutes, or until the peppers and onion are soft and the gnocchi is a little crispy.

4. Serve the gnocchi and veggies with the pesto for dipping, drizzled over the top, or tossed all together. Top with Parmesan, if desired.

NOTES

- If you can't find fresh refrigerated gnocchi, use shelf-stable gnocchi from the pasta aisle. Cook it according to the package directions, drain, and then toss with the roasted veggies.

- Use marinara sauce or Alfredo sauce for dipping. Warm for the best flavor.

- Serve with a side salad or Pan-Seared Chicken Tenders (page 238), if desired.

- Skip the onion and tomatoes to make this a little easier to prepare.

- Try Homemade Pesto (page 47).

Pick a protein: Add a 14.5-ounce can of drained and rinsed white beans for more protein.

PEPPERONI BREAD

PREP TIME: 10 minutes

COOK TIME: 26 minutes

TOTAL TIME: 36 minutes

16-ounce ball pizza dough
(see page 134)

4 ounces thinly sliced
pepperoni

3 cups shredded
mozzarella cheese

¼ cup grated
Parmesan cheese

1 tablespoon olive oil

1 teaspoon pizza seasoning
or Italian seasoning

Pizza sauce or marinara
sauce for dipping
(optional)

When I was growing up in New Jersey, Pepperoni Bread was a staple. And while I cannot fully replicate the flavor of the bread from my hometown pizza place, this is a close second. Plus it works equally well with a store-bought ball of pizza dough or a homemade dough. It's a fun way to change up pizza night, especially with a side of warmed pizza sauce for dipping and a simple side salad.

1. Preheat the oven to 425°F.

2. Place a big piece of parchment paper on a clean work surface. Using your hands, gently coax the pizza dough into a rectangle that's about 12 by 18 inches. (It's okay if it's not perfect.) Layer on the pepperoni, mozzarella, and Parmesan, leaving about an inch around the edge uncovered.

3. Starting at one long end of the dough, roll it up into a spiral, using the parchment paper to help lift and roll. Gently fold over the ends of the dough (this keeps the filling from seeping out of the sides). Transfer the dough, still on the parchment paper, to a half-sheet pan.

4. Brush the top of the dough with the olive oil and sprinkle with the pizza seasoning.

5. Bake the roll for 24 to 26 minutes, or until golden brown. Let cool for 3 to 5 minutes.

6. Slice the bread with a serrated knife and serve with pizza sauce for dipping, if desired.

NOTES

• We usually have this with Caesar salad, but do what you like.

• Spread a very thin layer of pizza sauce under the pepperoni to add more flavor to the inside.

Make it vegetarian:
Substitute sliced mushrooms or minced broccoli for the pepperoni.

HOMEMADE PIZZA DOUGH
MAKES: ABOUT 16 OUNCES

1 cup warm water, plus more
    as needed

2 teaspoons instant yeast

1 teaspoon granulated sugar

2 cups all-purpose flour

1 cup whole-wheat flour

2 tablespoons olive oil

1 teaspoon fine sea salt

Two hours to eight hours before you plan to bake the dough (in the morning works well), in a small bowl, combine the water, yeast, and sugar and stir gently. In a large bowl, combine the all-purpose flour, whole-wheat flour, olive oil, and salt. When the yeast is puffy, stir the mixture into the flour, then knead gently with your hands to bring the dough together. Add a little more water if needed to make the dough a little sticky but easy to work with. Cover with a clean kitchen towel and let sit at room temperature until ready to use.

CHOCOLATE CHIP PANCAKES

We love breakfast for dinner on Friday nights, on the weekend, or just on nights when cooking a "real" dinner seems like too much. And by baking a whole pan of pancakes at once, you can avoid the endless standing by the stove that comes with making traditional pancakes. These are fluffy and easy to slice into squares. Serve with fruit, maple syrup, and bacon or sausage, as your family prefers. Photograph on pages 136–137

SERVES: 4

PREP TIME: 10 minutes

COOK TIME: 14 minutes

TOTAL TIME: 24 minutes

½ cup plain yogurt

½ cup whole milk

2 eggs

2 tablespoons unsalted butter, melted and cooled slightly

1 cup all-purpose flour

1 tablespoon granulated sugar

2 teaspoons baking powder

¼ teaspoon fine sea salt

½ cup mini chocolate chips

Maple syrup, berries, and/or whipped cream for serving (optional)

1. Preheat the oven to 400°F. Line a quarter-sheet pan with parchment paper and coat the sides of the pan with nonstick spray to help prevent sticking.

2. In a medium bowl, combine the yogurt, milk, eggs, and butter and whisk for about 30 seconds until the mixture is smooth.

3. Add the flour, sugar, baking powder, and salt to the bowl and gently whisk to combine into a batter.

4. Pour the batter on the prepared pan and, using a spatula, spread gently to the edges. Sprinkle the chocolate chips evenly on top.

5. Bake the pancake for 12 to 14 minutes, or until lightly golden brown and just firm to the touch.

6. Slice the pancake and serve with your choice of toppings.

NOTES

• Use whole-wheat flour or gluten-free flour blend in place of all-purpose flour. The substitution is cup for cup.

• Add a dash of cinnamon and vanilla extract for more flavor.

• Cook the batter in a nonstick or cast-iron skillet on the stove as you would regular pancakes. Just melt a little butter in the pan to make sure the pancakes don't stick while cooking.

• To make this on a half-sheet pan, line it with parchment paper and spread the batter out until about ½ inch thick. It's okay that it doesn't cover the whole pan, although you can double the recipe and spread to the edges.

• Stir ½ cup blueberries or diced strawberries into the batter to vary the flavor of this recipe.

Chocolate Chip Pancakes, page 135

BAKED "GRILLED" CHEESE WITH HAM

You can make grilled cheese for the whole family in one fell swoop by baking the sandwiches together on a sheet pan—no standing by the stove cooking one or two at time! Dice or slice these up for younger eaters to make chewing easier, and add a simple side of applesauce, broccoli, or sliced fruit to round out the meal.

SERVES: 6

PREP TIME: 10 minutes

COOK TIME: 10 minutes

TOTAL TIME: 20 minutes

12 slices whole-grain or sourdough sandwich bread

8 tablespoons unsalted butter

6 to 12 slices cheddar cheese or American cheese

6 to 12 thin slices ham

1. Preheat the oven to 425°F. Line a half-sheet pan with parchment paper.

2. Spread one side of each bread slice with the butter. Place 6 slices, butter-side down, in the prepared pan. Top with the cheese and ham slices. (Use 1 or 2 slices of each depending on how much filling you like.) Top with the remaining bread slices, butter-side up.

3. Bake the sandwiches for 6 minutes and then carefully flip them with a spatula. Bake for 4 to 6 minutes more, or until the bread is golden brown and the cheese is melted. Remove from the oven and let cool for a minute or two.

4. Slice the sandwiches, if desired, before serving.

NOTES

- We like these sandwiches with a side of fruit or a big salad. Adults may like them with pickles and spicy mustard.

- If you have a big electric griddle, you can cook the sandwiches on that and skip heating up the oven too.

Make it vegetarian: Omit the ham, if desired.

Add a veggie: Using kitchen scissors, shred a few baby spinach leaves to place over the cheese and ham inside each sandwich before cooking.

HOW TO WASTE LESS FOOD
(AND USE UP WHAT YOU BUY)

There are three factors that impact potential food waste in my home: How much food we buy. What type of food we choose at the store. And how we actually offer the food to the kids. With the first two factors in mind, know that there are some easy ways to minimize food waste before you even get to your house.

Buy mostly the food you know your family likes. There is so much pressure placed on eating a "variety of foods," but there's really nothing wrong with making the core of your family's food purchases the reliable basics that your people prefer. You can buy much smaller amounts of new foods to try, which decreases the potential for wasted food. And consider "variety" over a much longer span of time.

Rely on fresh produce at the beginning of the week and then frozen, canned, and dried produce for later. You'll buy less fresh produce overall—which minimizes the quantity that may spoil before you have a chance to eat it—but you also have a stock of shelf-stable options for pinch-hitting.

There are so many amazing options in the freezer aisle. Since fruits and veggies are frozen at peak freshness, they may even taste better than fresh. And if you don't use some one week, no big deal—they can stay put until next week! (I love having a lot of produce options, but it's key to be realistic about how much fresh produce you can actually get through before it spoils.)

Make sure that the fresh produce you *do* buy is dry for storage. I place a paper towel inside any bags of lettuce or precut veggies

to absorb excess moisture that can cause these foods to spoil more quickly. You can fold up a paper towel, place it into a raspberry or strawberry container, and then flip the package over so the paper towel absorbs any moisture droplets that could encourage mold to grow. Store grapes in a wide bowl lined with a clean kitchen towel to keep them dry.

Choose produce that works for your current phase of life. This may mean using more frozen veggies to minimize chopping or getting that salad kit with the dressing and croutons that the kids love. Maybe it means splurging on precut pineapple once a week or thawing frozen mango to serve as a side rather than dealing with cutting up fresh fruit.

There is no right way to do any of this, so use the options that help you simplify!

Keep track of your leftovers and freezer stash. Institute one night each week when dinner is a "fridge forage" type of meal. This can be a great way to encourage everyone to eat what's already prepared and might otherwise be ignored.

How you present food to the kids is the third factor for cutting waste. So whenever you serve food, start with small portions for the kids to minimize the potential for waste from the get-go. Then, always try to allow seconds (and thirds) according to their hunger . . . assuming everyone has already had firsts!

TACOS
& BURRITOS

It's possible that I will look back at the early years of my kids' lives as the "taco years" simply due to the volume of tacos (and quesadillas and burritos) that we ate as a family. I don't know how I wound up with three kids who love tortillas, beans, and cheese as much as mine do, but it is what it is. (And I'm glad for this simple joy!) We rotate through all sorts of combinations of these foods and have a handful of favorites. The good news is that the base ingredients of this category of food are very straightforward and are so easy to change up according to the season or what you have on hand to use.

There are ideas here for fast tacos with all sorts of proteins, quesadillas with loads of veggies, and some burritos with satisfying fillings. In most cases, you can choose the type of tortilla that your family prefers, whether corn, flour, another grain, or a blend. That said, it's usually easier to make burritos using flour tortillas as they tend to crack and break less when rolling. And it's always easier to roll or fold any kind of tortilla if you warm it a little bit first.

For littler kids who are still learning to chew, know that you can always serve the components of these recipes side by side with thin strips of tortillas. Kitchen scissors are an easy way to make quick work of that!

SALSA-SHRIMP TACOS

SERVES: 4 TO 6

PREP TIME: 10 minutes

COOK TIME: 8 minutes

TOTAL TIME: 18 minutes

1 tablespoon olive oil

1 pound fresh or frozen shrimp, peeled and deveined

¼ cup mild salsa

¼ teaspoon fine sea salt

10 taco-size tortillas

One 16-ounce bag frozen sweet corn

Shredded cabbage, shredded cheese, hot sauce, fresh lime, and guacamole for topping (optional)

There are a few sauces that I like to keep on hand to eliminate the need for a bunch of other herbs and spices, and jarred salsa is one of them. Any kind works, and there are so many delicious options at the store—it's a perfect shortcut that adds a lot of flavor. For this recipe, I recommend using a salsa that is pureed smooth (I sometimes quickly blend a chunky store-bought salsa for this) so it evenly coats the shrimp.

1. In a large skillet over medium heat, warm the olive oil and swirl to coat the pan.

2. Add the shrimp to the skillet and cook for 3 minutes. Flip them and add the salsa and salt and cook for 3 to 5 minutes more, or until the shrimp are completely opaque. (It depends on the size of the shrimp—smaller ones cook faster.)

3. Meanwhile, wrap the tortillas in a damp, clean kitchen towel and microwave on full power for 30 seconds to warm. Flip the stack and microwave for 30 seconds more. Wrap the whole stack in a dry towel to keep the heat in. (You can also place the stack in a tortilla warmer and microwave for 60 seconds.)

4. Place the corn in a bowl and warm in the microwave according to the package directions.

5. Set the tortillas, shrimp, corn, and your choice of toppings on the table and let everyone build their own tacos.

NOTES

- If using frozen shrimp, thaw them according to the package directions before starting the recipe.

- If you want to save a bowl, add the corn to the skillet to cook with the shrimp.

- If you can only find shrimp that has the shell and tail on (or if it's less expensive to buy it that way), that is totally fine. You just need to clean them before you start.

- Cut the shrimp into very small bite-size pieces for younger eaters to ensure that it's easy to chew.

FISH-STICK TACOS

PREP TIME: 5 minutes

COOK TIME: 15 minutes

TOTAL TIME: 20 minutes

1 pound frozen fish sticks

8 to 12 taco-size tortillas

½ cup mild salsa

½ cup sour cream

Shredded lettuce, shredded cheese, diced avocado, chopped tomato, and hot sauce for topping (optional)

Yes, I do sometimes make homemade fish sticks (see page 148), but on busy weeknights, frozen is usually the way to go. Plus, the texture and crunch are always perfect and there's no need to dirty a sink of dishes. The crispy fish sticks are so, so good with the soft tortillas and the fresh (always optional) toppings of avocado, tomato, and lettuce. Add a side of fruit or a Mexican-style salad kit to round out this meal.

1. Cook the fish sticks according to the package directions.

2. Wrap the tortillas in a damp, clean kitchen towel and microwave on full power for 30 seconds to warm. Flip the stack and microwave for 30 seconds more. Wrap the whole stack in a dry towel to keep the heat in. (You can also place the stack in a tortilla warmer and microwave for 60 seconds.)

3. In a small bowl, combine the salsa and sour cream and stir to make a quick dipping sauce.

4. Place the fish sticks, tortillas, and your choice of toppings on the table. Let everyone assemble their own tacos, with the sauce on top or on the side.

NOTES

- If you decide to put a little more muscle into preparation, forgo the frozen fish and opt for Homemade Fish Sticks instead.

- Top the tacos with a coleslaw mix for extra crunch.

- Make it a taco salad by serving the components over a base of shredded lettuce.

- Add guacamole, sour cream, lime, and any other toppings you prefer.

HOMEMADE FISH STICKS

MAKES: 1 POUND

1 pound tilapia fillets
⅓ cup all-purpose flour
2 eggs, lightly beaten

1¼ cups panko breadcrumbs
Fine sea salt

Preheat the oven to 425°F. Line a rimmed half-sheet pan with aluminum foil or parchment paper and coat with nonstick spray. Cut the tilapia into finger-size pieces. (Using kitchen scissors makes this quick.) Place the flour, eggs, and panko in three separate, wide bowls. Coat each piece of fish in the flour, the eggs, and then the panko. Place in the prepared pan, season with salt, and bake for 10 to 12 minutes. Use immediately.

LAMB TACOS WITH YOGURT SAUCE

PREP TIME: 10 minutes

COOK TIME: 12 minutes

TOTAL TIME: 22 minutes

2 tablespoons olive oil

1 pound ground lamb

1 small yellow onion, minced

2 garlic cloves, minced,
 or 1 teaspoon garlic
 powder

1 teaspoon oregano

½ teaspoon fine sea salt

12 taco-size tortillas

4- to 8-ounce container
 tzatziki sauce or 1 cup
 Homemade Yogurt Sauce
 (recipe follows)

Sliced avocado, tomato,
 and cucumber for serving
 (optional)

Make it faster: Use frozen minced onion to make this a little easier or, if you prefer, you can peel the onion and then grate it on a box grater for smaller pieces that disappear into the ground meat.

Every once in a while, especially in spring, we buy lamb from a local farmer to make these Greek-style tacos. They cook up really quickly and have subtle spices that pair particularly well with the flavor of the meat. We usually have warmed and buttered frozen corn or a salad kit on the side. Add some sliced avocado, tomato, and cucumbers as toppings. Photograph on pages 150–151

1. In a medium skillet over medium heat, warm the olive oil. Add the lamb, using a wooden spoon to break it up. Add the onion, garlic, oregano, and salt; stir to coat; and cook for 8 to 10 minutes, or until the lamb is browned completely and the onion is very soft. Drain any excess liquid as needed.

2. Meanwhile, wrap the tortillas in a damp, clean kitchen towel and microwave on full power for 30 seconds to warm. Flip the stack and microwave for 30 seconds more. Wrap the whole stack in a dry towel to keep the heat in. (You can also place the stack in a tortilla warmer and microwave for 60 seconds.)

3. Set the lamb, tortillas, tzatziki, and your choice of toppings on the table and let everyone build their own tacos.

NOTES

- Use ground beef or chicken or firm tofu, drained and crumbled, instead of lamb.

- Serve the mixture with rice as a meal-in-a-bowl option.

- Swap in pita or flatbread for the tortillas.

HOMEMADE YOGURT SAUCE

MAKES: ABOUT 1 CUP

½ cup plain Greek yogurt

½ cup cucumber, minced

1 tablespoon lemon juice

⅛ teaspoon fine sea salt

In a small bowl, combine the yogurt, cucumber, lemon juice, and salt and stir to incorporate. Store in an airtight container in the fridge for up to 5 days.

Lamb Tacos with Yogurt Sauce
page 149

CHICKEN-TENDER TACOS

Crispy chicken, soft tortillas, flavorful salsa—it's a simple combination that's seriously satisfying. You can use frozen, prepared chicken tenders or you can make them from scratch yourself. Both work and are yummy. I love keeping frozen ones on hand as a fast option for busy nights.

SERVES: 4 TO 6

PREP TIME: 10 minutes

COOK TIME: 10 minutes

TOTAL TIME: 20 minutes

12 taco-size tortillas

1 pound cooked frozen breaded chicken strips or Homemade Crispy Chicken Tenders (facing page), cut into thin pieces or shredded

1 cup shredded lettuce

Shredded cheese, fresh cilantro, salsa, guacamole, and sour cream for topping (optional)

1. Wrap the tortillas in a damp, clean kitchen towel and microwave on full power for 30 seconds to warm. Flip the stack and microwave for 30 seconds more. Wrap the whole stack in a dry towel to keep the heat in. (You can also place the stack in a tortilla warmer and microwave for 60 seconds.)

2. Set the tortillas, chicken, lettuce, and your choice of toppings on the table and let everyone build their own tacos.

NOTES

• Serve the components of this taco meal side by side for younger eaters. This ensures it's easy for them to pick up the taco and to eat it.

• Swap in a plant-based tender or nugget if you prefer.

Add a veggie: When cooking the chicken, in a separate baking pan, cook roasted broccoli (see page 243). Place the pan on the rack below the chicken tenders to efficiently cook both side and main dishes.

HOMEMADE CRISPY CHICKEN TENDERS

MAKES: 1 POUND

⅓ cup all-purpose flour

1 egg, lightly beaten

1 cup bread crumbs

1 pound chicken tenders

2 tablespoons olive oil or unsalted butter

Fine sea salt

Cumin for sprinkling

1. Put the flour, egg, and bread crumbs in separate bowls. Dip the tenders first in the flour, then the egg, and then into the bread crumbs. Set aside on a plate.

2. In a large skillet over medium heat, warm the olive oil.

3. Add the chicken to the skillet and sprinkle with salt and cumin. Cover and cook for 4 minutes, flip the chicken, and then cook for 3 to 4 minutes more, or until a meat thermometer registers 165°F. Use immediately.

OVEN VERSION

Coat a baking pan with cooking spray, add the prepared chicken, and bake in a 425°F oven for 14 to 16 minutes, turning halfway through.

AIR-FRYER VERSION

In a 400°F air fryer, cook for 8 to 10 minutes, turning halfway through.

HUEVOS-RANCHEROS TACOS

Eggs are one of those staples that we always have on hand. And since they're an affordable protein option, we often have them as a taco filling. We like these with corn tortillas, but you can use any kind that your family enjoys. I cook both the peppers and the eggs in the same pan to minimize cleanup. These are a yummy breakfast taco to share any time of the day.

SERVES: 4 TO 6

PREP TIME: 10 minutes

COOK TIME: 15 minutes

TOTAL TIME: 25 minutes

2 tablespoons unsalted butter or a neutral oil (such as canola or avocado)

2 medium bell peppers (any color), cored, seeded, and thinly sliced

½ teaspoon taco seasoning

8 eggs, lightly beaten

One 14.5-ounce can beans (such as black or pinto), drained and rinsed

12 taco-size tortillas

Salsa, shredded cheese, sour cream, and other taco garnishes for topping (optional)

Make it egg-free: Use a 16-ounce block of drained and diced firm tofu in place of the eggs.

1. In a large nonstick or cast-iron skillet over medium heat, melt 1 tablespoon of the butter. Add the bell peppers and taco seasoning and cook, stirring occasionally, for 10 to 12 minutes, or until just soft. Transfer the peppers to a plate and cover with another plate to keep warm.

2. In the same skillet over medium heat, melt the remaining 1 tablespoon butter. Swirl to coat the bottom of the pan. Add the eggs, stirring occasionally to allow the uncooked eggs to flow under the cooked mixture, and cook for 4 to 6 minutes, or until cooked through.

3. In a microwave-safe bowl, microwave the beans on full power for 1 to 2 minutes, or until heated through.

4. Wrap the tortillas in a damp, clean kitchen towel and microwave on full power for 30 seconds to warm. Flip the stack and microwave for 30 seconds more. Wrap the whole stack in a dry towel to keep the heat in. (You can also place the stack in a tortilla warmer and microwave for 60 seconds.)

5. Set the eggs, peppers, beans, tortillas, and your choice of toppings on the table and let everyone build their own tacos.

NOTES

- If the kids don't want *every* component of the meal, that's totally normal—and it's actually okay. Most kids eat a much wider variety of foods than we realize if we look at their food intake over the course of a whole week rather than at any one dinner.

- If you don't have taco seasoning, use ½ teaspoon cumin, ¼ teaspoon chili powder, ¼ teaspoon garlic powder, and ¼ teaspoon salt.

- Stir a little salsa into the black beans to add flavor, if desired.

SAUSAGE & EGG BREAKFAST BURRITOS

When we want a change from our usual bean burritos, these are a favorite option. Simply combine scrambled eggs, breakfast sausage, and cheese for a mixture that's, quite frankly, delicious at any time of the day. I prefer to use fajita-size tortillas as I find that the slightly smaller size works better for my family, but you can scale this up or down as you like.

SERVES: 4 TO 6

PREP TIME: 10 minutes

COOK TIME: 10 minutes

TOTAL TIME: 20 minutes

1 tablespoon
    unsalted butter

8 eggs

1 pound cooked breakfast
    sausage (fresh or frozen),
    cut into ½-inch rounds

½ cup shredded
    cheddar cheese

6 fajita-size tortillas

Sour cream, salsa, and
    guacamole for topping
    (optional)

Add a veggie: In Step 4, add 1 to 2 cups diced roasted sweet potato (see page 244) or warmed frozen corn to the egg mixture in the pan.

1. In a large nonstick or cast-iron skillet over medium heat, melt the butter. Using a spatula, swirl the butter to cover the pan's bottom surface.

2. Crack the eggs into a large bowl or liquid measuring cup and whisk to break up the yolks. Pour into the melted butter and let set for 1 minute. Then, using the spatula, gently push the cooked part of the egg to allow the uncooked egg to flow underneath. Continue to gently scramble the eggs for 4 to 6 minutes, allowing them to cook evenly, until they're cooked through.

3. Add the sausage and cheese to the eggs, stir gently to combine, and then turn off the heat.

4. Wrap the tortillas in a damp, clean kitchen towel and microwave on full power for 30 seconds to warm. Flip the stack and microwave for 30 seconds more. Wrap the whole stack in a dry towel to keep the heat in. (You can also place the stack in a tortilla warmer and microwave for 60 seconds.)

5. Working with one tortilla at a time, place ½ cup of the egg mixture in the middle, fold over two sides of the burrito, and then roll up from one of the remaining sides. Place each burrito seam-side down on a plate or baking dish.

6. Serve the burritos, warm, with your choice of toppings.

NOTES

• Serve with hash browns, fruit, or applesauce.

• Add diced avocado to each burrito, if desired.

• Use any flavor of breakfast sausage you prefer. (I like chicken maple.)

QUICK RICE & BEAN BURRITOS

PREP TIME: 10 minutes

COOK TIME: 12 minutes

TOTAL TIME: 22 minutes

2 cups cooked brown rice

One 14.5-ounce can black beans, drained and rinsed

½ cup shredded cheddar cheese

½ cup smooth-style salsa, plus more for topping (optional)

6 fajita-size tortillas

Sour cream and guacamole for topping (optional)

Add a veggie: In a skillet over medium heat, warm 1 teaspoon olive oil. Add 2 cups frozen bell pepper strips (any color) or frozen sweet corn and cook for 6 to 8 minutes, or until the vegetables are soft. Stir this into the mixture in Step 2 and increase the number of tortillas to eight as this makes a slightly larger batch.

Stirring together a handful of precooked ingredients is a fast way to make a batch of seriously satisfying burritos. We usually use black beans for these, but pinto beans would also work well. You can serve them plain or add bell peppers and corn to the mix along with some dipping sauces and a side of fruit (like mango or pineapple), and dinner is done. (I often double this recipe so I have a second batch ready for lunch the following day.) Look for fully cooked rice in your supermarket, or make it from scratch, transfer to an airtight container and store in the fridge for up to 5 days.

1. Preheat the oven to 375°F. Line a baking sheet with aluminum foil or parchment paper. Set aside.

2. In a medium bowl, combine the rice, beans, cheese, and salsa and stir to incorporate.

3. Working with one tortilla at a time, place on a microwave-safe plate and top with ½ cup of the bean mixture. Microwave on full power for 30 seconds to warm.

4. Fold over two sides of the tortilla and then roll up from one of the remaining sides. Place each burrito seam-side down on the prepared baking sheet.

5. Place the burritos in the oven for 8 to 10 minutes, or until warm.

6. Serve the burritos with your choice of toppings.

NOTES

- You can make these ahead to avoid some dinnertime prep. After completing Step 4, cover the burritos and store in the fridge for up to 4 hours. Bake at 375°F for 10 to 12 minutes, or until warmed through.

- Add thawed frozen corn, shredded baby spinach, or shredded cooked chicken to the mixture.

- At Step 5, you can warm in the microwave (instead of the oven) for 30 to 60 seconds.

REFRIED BEAN BURRITOS

PREP TIME: 10 minutes

COOK TIME: 8 minutes

TOTAL TIME: 18 minutes

8 fajita-size tortillas

One 14.5-ounce can refried beans or 1 recipe Homemade Refried Beans (page 164)

One 14.5-ounce can sweet corn, drained and rinsed

2 cups shredded cheddar cheese

Cumin for sprinkling

2 cups shredded lettuce

1 cup pico de gallo or chunky-style salsa (optional)

Pick a protein: Add shredded chicken or cooked ground beef to the burritos.

This recipe—which is really more of a method—was the first way that my little guy ever tried a burrito . . . in part, I think, because I let him make his himself. (Whenever someone asks how they can help their child try new foods, one of my first answers is always to try to give the kids a little more power and control over their plate.) There is, of course, no guarantee that giving kids the chance to help cook will increase the number of foods they like, but it certainly might. Start with canned refried beans to keep this fast or make them yourself using whole beans.

1. Place the tortillas in an even layer on a clean counter or work surface.

2. Put ¼ cup beans, ¼ cup corn, ¼ cup cheese, and a sprinkle of cumin down the center of each tortilla.

3. Working one at a time, place a tortilla (with fillings) on a heat-safe plate. Microwave on full power for 30 to 60 seconds, or until the cheese is melted.

4. Add a little lettuce and pico de gallo (if using) on top of the filling, fold over two sides of the burrito, and then roll up from one of the remaining sides. Place each burrito seam-side down on a plate or baking dish.

5. Serve the burritos warm.

NOTES

• Let the kids make their own burritos—if you have the time and patience!

• Use whole-wheat or gluten-free tortillas as you like.

• Replace the refried beans with regular beans if you prefer. Mash them slightly if you want to make them a little more likely to stay put in the tortilla.

HOMEMADE REFRIED BEANS

MAKES: ABOUT 2½ CUPS

One 14.5-ounce can pinto
beans, drained and rinsed

½ cup warm water or
reduced-sodium chicken
stock or vegetable stock

1 teaspoon cumin

½ teaspoon oregano

½ teaspoon chili powder

¼ teaspoon fine sea salt

Place the beans in a large bowl or food processor. Add the warm water, cumin, oregano, chili powder, and salt and then mash with a potato masher or process until very smooth. Store in an airtight container in the fridge for up to 5 days.

BLACK BEAN & CORN QUESADILLAS

Baking a big batch of quesadillas on baking sheets decreases the amount of time you have to stand by the stove. The flavor and texture at the end are nearly identical too. Win! (You can make this recipe on a big electric griddle, if you prefer.) Serve with a side of warmed, frozen sweet corn or Roasted Carrots (page 240). Photograph on pages 166–167

Photograph on pages 166–167

SERVES: 4 TO 6

PREP TIME: 10 minutes

COOK TIME: 8 minutes

TOTAL TIME: 18 minutes

8 fajita-size tortillas

One 28.5-ounce can black beans, drained and rinsed

One 14.5-ounce can sweet corn, drained and rinsed

2 cups shredded cheddar cheese

1 teaspoon cumin

½ teaspoon chili powder

Salsa, guacamole, and sour cream for topping (optional)

1. Preheat the oven to 375°F. Line two baking sheets with aluminum foil or parchment paper.

2. Lay the tortillas on the prepared baking sheets. Place about ¼ cup beans on half of each tortilla. Top each with a little corn, cheese, cumin, and chili powder.

3. Bake the quesadillas for 4 minutes and then fold over the empty side of the tortilla to make a half-moon shape. Using a spatula, press down and flip each quesadilla. Bake for 3 to 4 minutes more, or until the cheese is melted through.

4. Serve the quesadillas, warm, with your choice of toppings.

NOTES

• Use pinto beans instead of black beans.

• Add cooked, chopped broccoli florets, roasted sweet potato cubes, or another cooked veggie, if desired.

• Use corn or flour tortillas, though know that ones labeled "soft" tend to work best in this recipe.

Black Bean & Corn Quesadillas,
page 165

SPINACH QUESADILLAS

SERVES: 4 TO 6

PREP TIME: 10 minutes

COOK TIME: 4 minutes

TOTAL TIME: 14 minutes

10 fajita-size tortillas

1 cup shredded
cheddar cheese

2 tablespoons sour cream,
cream cheese, or plain
Greek yogurt

¼ teaspoon cumin

⅛ teaspoon chili powder

2 cups spinach

Salsa for dipping (optional)

This creamy filling is a delicious way to change up classic quesadillas and is also just a yummy way to serve greens to the family. There are two methods for preparing this—by stirring the ingredients in a bowl or blending them more finely in a food processor. Both are great options, with the first being a little faster and less fussy and the latter being the way to add a lot more greens. (P.S. This also makes a seriously delish filling for grilled cheese!)

1. Place the tortillas in an even layer on a clean counter or work surface.

2. In a small bowl, combine the cheese, sour cream, cumin, and chili powder and stir to incorporate. Spread the cheese mixture on half of each tortilla. Lay a few spinach leaves on top, overlapping them a little.

3. Set a large skillet over medium heat. When warm, place each tortilla in the skillet, filling-side up. (You may need to work with a few at a time.) Cook for 2 minutes, fold over the empty half to make a half-moon shape, and flip them. Cook for 2 minutes more.

4. Serve the quesadillas, warm, with salsa for dipping, if desired.

NOTES

- Use baby kale instead of spinach, if you prefer.

- Use nondairy shredded cheese and sour cream as desired.

- Tortillas made of flour or a corn-flour blend are usually the softest kind and the easiest to use when making these quesadillas. They are less likely than corn tortillas to crack or break when you fold them.

- You can also add a full 5-ounce bag of spinach to a food processor with the rest of the ingredients. Grind into a thick mixture and spread on the tortillas.

THE
MAGIC
OF FAMILY-
STYLE
MEALS

There's been a lot of buzz in the last few years about the concept of "family style" meals as a magical way to improve "picky eating." While I do think that this approach to feeding can help, I want to say right up front that it's not magic. It is, however, one tool to have in your arsenal that may improve mealtime dynamics.

The way that I think of *family style* means that we put all the food for a meal on the table. This allows everyone to see what's on offer and makes it easy for kids to have seconds (and thirds) without a parent needing to get up from their own meal—which, I am sure we can all agree, is a worthwhile and amazing goal. This also helps kids learn to serve themselves; that can go a long way toward making them feel more in control of their own food.

I started offering meals family-style because it's how our daycare served things. I saw classrooms full of one-year-olds participating—scooping out food to put on their own plates. This, done from a young age, can have kids participating in a meal in a way that plays to their desire to do it all themselves. We followed that example and started to do the same thing at home. We realized quickly that this helped our then toddler be more in charge of what wound up on her plate, which made her (and us) happier.

We love doing this because it's one of the easiest ways to serve a meal to a diverse mix of people while still letting everyone have the specific mix of foods that they prefer on their plate. In other words, it eliminates the pressure on a parent or care provider to read the mind (or tummy) of any other person and instead hands that responsibility over to each individual. This works well with the concept known as the Division of Responsibility in Feeding, which was developed by feeding therapist Ellyn Satter. This approach has the parents in charge of the *what*, the *when*, and the *how* of meals—so they decide what's offered, at what time, and where the meal happens. And then everyone at the table gets to decide *which* foods they want and *how much* to eat.

For me, this fosters bodily autonomy from an early age and allows each person to enjoy their meal and learn the unique cues of their own hunger and fullness signals. (And I really like that I can customize my own plate for my taste too.) Kids' appetites and preferences can shift so much as they grow that it can be really frustrating to constantly try to guess how much food they need or which foods they might like on any particular day. The family-style approach takes this stress off the parent's shoulders and lets the kid be in charge of those aspects, which is a great thing for them to learn because it's exactly what we want them to be able to do when they're out in the world eating without us, like at daycare, preschool, elementary school, and beyond. I do remind the kids that we all need to share— because there certainly are times when one child wants the entire bowl of cheese. And we do our best as parents to encourage the kids to try other foods if their favorites have been eaten so we aren't being pressured to get up and make more of anything.

The one downside of family-style meals is that sometimes they generate a lot of dishes or a little pressure to offer a lot of options.

Whenever possible, I simply put the food on the table in the vessel that I cooked it in, use big platters or trays if I'm serving something such as a big salad with a few components, and remind myself that sides and toppings can be super-simple. Family-style does not mean that you need to have every condiment or side dish possibility in the house on the table at the same time. It works with a single skillet meal just as well as with burrito bowls. It's simply a way to put the food in a place where everyone can easily access it.

This may or may not work for your phase of life right now. But it can be a consideration if you're looking for ways to reset the dynamics of family meals gone awry.

SKILLET MEALS

I often joke that every recipe should come with a "dirty-dishes indicator" so we have an idea, right up front, of how many dirty dishes we might wind up with at the end. Rest assured that the recipes in this chapter are made in a single skillet or a saucepan. You might need some measuring spoons and a knife here and there, but you won't wind up with a tower of pots to scrub at the end of the night. (I can feel your relief through the page!)

Because these include a lot of mixed-together foods, where possible, there are notes in each recipe on how to adjust for kids who prefer their foods to be separate. You may also be able to invite the kids to make choices about their meal to help them feel in control, even with mixed foods on the table. Let them choose which side to include, have them pick their plate and fork, let them try serving themselves, ask them what you can add to the meal to make it yummier. None of these are perfect solutions—many kids simply need to see foods a lot of times over a long span of time to gain confidence to eat it themselves—but they may help.

TOMATO-BRAISED FISH WITH COUSCOUS

With subtle North African flavors from cumin and cinnamon, this 15-minute fish dish is one that I turn to when I want to change up which protein we're eating. It's also a nutritious meal that's packed with fancy-tasting flavors. This is quick to make with couscous, but any grain will work. We usually include sliced cucumbers and plain yogurt on the table to serve as toppings and as safety nets for anyone who isn't into the entree. I use a nonstick skillet for this recipe, but a stainless-steel pan will work too.

SERVES: 4 TO 6

PREP TIME: 5 minutes

COOK TIME: 10 minutes

TOTAL TIME: 15 minutes

1½ cups couscous

2 cups boiling water

2 tablespoons olive oil or unsalted butter

1 teaspoon cumin

½ teaspoon cinnamon

½ teaspoon sweet paprika

½ teaspoon garlic powder

One 8-ounce can tomato sauce

¼ cup golden raisins or regular raisins

1 pound fresh or frozen tilapia fillets

Fine sea salt

Finely grated lemon zest and cilantro for topping (optional)

1. In a medium heat-safe bowl, top the couscous with the boiling water. (The couscous absorbs the water and is cooked by the time you're done cooking the fish.)

2. In a medium skillet over medium heat, warm the olive oil. Add the cumin, cinnamon, paprika, and garlic powder; stir; and cook for 1 minute. Add the tomato sauce and raisins, stir, and bring to a simmer.

3. Add the fish to the skillet, turn the heat to medium-low, and cook for 3 minutes. Gently flip the fish and cook for 3 to 4 minutes more, or until it is opaque and cooked through. Sprinkle with salt.

4. Fluff the couscous with a fork.

5. Serve the fish over the couscous with your choice of toppings.

NOTES

- Skip the couscous and try rice or pasta instead. Or omit the grain and serve with toast.

- Use shrimp or another favorite fish instead of tilapia. You may need to lengthen the cooking time if the fish is thicker. I like tilapia because it's affordable and usually a more sustainable option than many other similar fish. Or, swap in two cans of drained and rinsed chickpeas.

- To use frozen fish, thaw according to the package directions and proceed as directed.

- No paprika? No problem. Just skip it!

TIKKA MASALA CHICKEN & CAULIFLOWER

Jarred simmer sauces are one of my favorite ways to get the perfect flavor you'd expect from takeout, but for less cost—and often more speed. Paired with naan bread and some sliced cucumbers, this is a quick and satisfying meal. Chicken thighs are incredibly tender when simmered this way, so that is my top pick here. But know that you can use a different cut if you prefer.

SERVES: 4 TO 6

PREP TIME: 5 minutes

COOK TIME: 14 minutes

TOTAL TIME: 19 minutes

One 12.5-ounce jar tikka masala simmer sauce

1 pound chicken thighs

1 pound fresh or frozen cauliflower florets

8 ounces naan bread

Sliced cucumbers, plain Greek yogurt, and/or sour cream for topping (optional)

1. In a wide skillet over medium heat, warm the sauce. Add the chicken, spreading each thigh out flat, and top with the cauliflower. Cover and cook for 10 minutes.

2. Turn the chicken and stir gently to coat the cauliflower with the sauce. Re-cover and cook for 4 minutes more, or until the chicken is cooked through.

3. Place the naan on a microwave-safe plate and microwave on full power for 30 seconds to warm.

4. Serve the chicken and cauliflower with the naan on the side and your choice of toppings.

NOTES

- I like to use frozen cauliflower because it's convenient, but fresh works just about the same.

- Use chicken tenders instead of chicken thighs.

- If this is a new food for the kids, start with a very small portion and show them how to dip their bread into the sauce. Kids like to model what grown-ups do at the table . . . at least, sometimes!

Make it vegetarian: Use a 16-ounce block of extra-firm tofu, diced, instead of chicken thighs.

MEXICAN GROUND-BEEF SKILLET

There are few things more satisfying (to me, at least) than a skillet meal that's just as delicious when eaten with a spoon as it is as a dip for chips. This lightly spiced medley relies mostly on pantry staples but is easily freshened up with a sprinkle of fresh cilantro on top. You could even roll this up into burritos if that sounds good to you.

SERVES: 4 TO 6

PREP TIME: 10 minutes

COOK TIME: 15 minutes

TOTAL TIME: 25 minutes

1 tablespoon olive oil

1 garlic clove, peeled and minced, or ½ teaspoon jarred minced garlic

1 small white or yellow onion, peeled and grated, or ½ cup frozen minced onion

1 pound ground beef

2 teaspoons taco seasoning

One 8-ounce can tomato sauce

1 cup uncooked jasmine rice

One 14.5-ounce can reduced-sodium chicken stock or beef stock

One 12- to 14-ounce bag frozen corn

One 14.5-ounce can black beans, drained and rinsed

½ cup shredded cheddar cheese or Mexican cheese blend

Sour cream, fresh cilantro, sliced jalapeños, and diced tomatoes for topping (optional)

1. In a large skillet over medium-high heat, warm the olive oil Add the garlic and onion, stir, and cook for 2 minutes.

2. Add the beef to the skillet and, using a wooden spoon, break up the meat.

3. Stir the taco seasoning, tomato sauce, rice, and chicken stock into the meat and bring to a simmer.

4. Cover the skillet and cook for 12 to 15 minutes, or until the rice is fluffy and soft and the liquid is mostly absorbed. Then stir in the corn, beans, and cheese to warm through.

5. Serve the beef, warm, with your choice of toppings.

NOTES

- My kids don't like pieces of onion, so I grate the onion on a hand-held grater and it blends right in. If yours don't care, you can just dice it. You can also omit the fresh onion if you want to make this a little easier.

- No taco seasoning? No problem! Use 1 tablespoon cumin, 1 teaspoon chili powder, and ½ teaspoon garlic powder for similar flavor. Season with salt.

- Serve with tortilla chips, tortillas, or plantain chips, if you'd like.

- Replace the beef with ground chicken or ground turkey.

Make it vegetarian: Omit the beef and use two 14.5-ounce cans of black beans (drained and rinsed) instead and sub in a veggie stock for the chicken stock.

Add a veggie: In Step 3, add 1 to 2 cups frozen bell pepper slices to bring some color to this dish.

Skillet Chicken Enchiladas, page 182

SKILLET CHICKEN ENCHILADAS

Enchiladas are amazing, except for the whole labor-intensive multistep aspect. To address that issue, but still keep the flavor and texture, we simply stack the components in a skillet. The result? A delicious, layered enchilada that you can simply dish up with a big spoon. This is particularly good with a bowl of diced mango on the side. Photograph on page 181

SERVES: 4 TO 6

PREP TIME: 5 minutes

COOK TIME: 18 minutes

TOTAL TIME: 23 minutes

1 tablespoon olive oil

1 pound chicken thighs, trimmed of excess fat

One 8-ounce can red enchilada sauce

One 8-ounce can tomato sauce

6 corn tortillas, cut into bite-size pieces

One 14.5-ounce can black beans, drained and rinsed

One 14.5-ounce can sweet corn, drained and rinsed

1 cup shredded Mexican-blend cheese or cheddar cheese

Diced avocado, crushed tortilla chips, chopped fresh cilantro, and sliced jalapeños for topping (optional)

1. In a large skillet over medium-high heat, warm the olive oil. Add the chicken and cook for 4 minutes. Flip the chicken and cook for 4 minutes more, or until cooked through.

2. Using a pair of kitchen scissors, cut the chicken into bite-size pieces right in the pan.

3. Drizzle about one-third of the enchilada sauce and one-third of the tomato sauce over the chicken and then scatter half the tortilla pieces on top. (You need to overlap them a little.)

4. Add the beans, corn, and ½ cup of the cheese to the skillet. Drizzle about one-third of the enchilada sauce and one-third of the tomato sauce on top.

5. Top with the remaining tortilla pieces. Drizzle the final third of the enchilada sauce and the tomato sauce over the top and scatter with the remaining ½ cup cheese.

6. Cover the skillet and turn off the heat. Let sit for 5 minutes to warm through and melt the cheese. (Or you can put the pan, uncovered, under a broiler on high heat for 3 to 5 minutes to brown and melt the cheese.)

7. Serve the enchiladas with your choice of toppings.

NOTES

• I prefer to use mild enchilada sauce, but you can level up the heat if your family has a higher spice tolerance. Green or red sauce both work, so choose the one with the flavor you prefer. (Red sauce is usually smokier with chipotle chiles.)

• I quickly cut the tortillas with kitchen scissors.

Make it vegetarian:
Use a second 14.5-ounce can of black beans or two 14.5-ounce cans of pinto beans in place of the chicken.

BRAISED TERIYAKI TOFU & GREEN BEANS

Sautéing extra-firm tofu gives it a pleasing golden brown color and helps infuse it with a lot of flavor—which can make it more appealing to both kids and adults. In this dish, the tofu is paired with teriyaki sauce and green beans for flavor. You can top this meal with chopped peanuts or sesame seeds if you like and swap out the rice for Asian-style noodles of any kind. Photograph on pages 184–185

SERVES: 4

PREP TIME: 5 minutes

COOK TIME: 20 minutes

TOTAL TIME: 25 minutes

1½ cups uncooked jasmine rice or basmati rice

One 16-ounce block extra-firm tofu, drained and diced into 1-inch cubes

2 tablespoons toasted sesame oil or neutral oil (such as canola or avocado)

1 garlic clove, peeled and minced, or ½ teaspoon jarred minced garlic

1 teaspoon minced ginger or grated frozen ginger

1 pound green beans, trimmed

½ cup reduced-sodium chicken stock or vegetable stock

Sesame seeds or chopped peanuts for topping (optional)

Bottled reduced-sodium teriyaki sauce for drizzling

1. Cook the rice according to the package directions, or until it is soft and most of the liquid has been absorbed. Then turn off the heat, cover, and set aside.

2. Firmly press the tofu with a clean kitchen towel to absorb more of the water.

3. In a large skillet over medium heat, warm the sesame oil. Add the garlic and ginger and cook for about 1 minute, stirring a few times.

4. Add the tofu to the skillet and cook for 4 minutes. Flip it and cook for 4 minutes more.

5. Add the green beans and chicken stock to the skillet, cover, and cook for 10 minutes more, or until the green beans are just tender.

6. Serve the tofu and green beans over the rice. Add your choice of toppings and drizzle with teriyaki sauce.

NOTES

- Use broccoli florets instead of green beans, if desired.

- Use any grain you like, including quinoa, a different rice, or even soba or rice noodles.

- To save a step, use frozen fully cooked rice from the store and warm according to the package directions.

- If you don't have stock, use water.

Pick a protein: Use chicken tenders or shrimp in place of the tofu.

Braised Teriyaki Tofu & Green Beans,
page 183

SKILLET LASAGNA

SERVES: 4 TO 6

PREP TIME: 5 minutes

COOK TIME: 25 minutes

TOTAL TIME: 30 minutes

8 ounces lasagna noodles

One 25-ounce jar
 marinara sauce

1 cup water

1 cup ricotta cheese

1 cup shredded
 mozzarella cheese

¼ cup grated
 Parmesan cheese

Fresh chopped basil for
 topping (optional)

This lasagna is significantly faster to cook than the traditional kind that bakes in the oven, but if you close your eyes as you take a bite, you'll never be able to tell the difference. You get all the flavors and the texture contrast of the noodles and cheeses with much (much) less work . . . and just one pan to clean!

1. Break the lasagna noodles into bite-size pieces. (Helping with this may be fun for the kids!)

2. In a large skillet over medium-high heat, combine the marinara sauce and water and bring to a simmer.

3. Add the noodles to the skillet and stir to coat. Cover, turn the heat to medium-low, and cook, stirring once or twice, for 15 to 20 minutes, or until the noodles are just soft. (They may stick a little in the middle of the pan so be sure to stir them.)

4. Top with dollops of the ricotta and sprinkle with the mozzarella and Parmesan. Turn off the heat, cover, and let sit for 5 minutes to melt the cheese. Or place under a broiler on high heat for 3 to 5 minutes to melt the cheese and brown it slightly.

5. Top the lasagna with fresh basil, if desired, before serving.

NOTES

- Use a marinara sauce that you love—it's the primary flavoring in this recipe.

- At the end of Step 3, you can also stir in 1 cup cooked broccoli florets, cauliflower florets, or carrot rounds.

- You can make this with meat, if you like. Before starting Step 1, in a large skillet over medium-high heat, brown 1 pound of ground beef or ground sausage. Drain off any excess fat and continue as directed.

BREAKFAST-FOR-DINNER SKILLET

Want eggs, sausage, and hash browns . . . but with fewer pans and a faster method? Me too! This skillet is made of breakfast favorites but is a satisfying dinner you can pull together even when you're short on energy or time. I use frozen potatoes for ease since they're already peeled and diced and then add fruit and toast on the side to complete the meal.

SERVES: 4 TO 6

PREP TIME: 5 minutes

COOK TIME: 20 minutes

TOTAL TIME: 25 minutes

2 tablespoons unsalted butter

One 16-ounce bag frozen cubed hash brown potatoes

1 teaspoon dried rosemary, crushed

½ teaspoon cumin

½ teaspoon chili powder

½ teaspoon fine sea salt

8 ounces cooked breakfast sausage links, cut into ½-inch thick rounds

4 eggs

½ cup shredded cheddar cheese (optional)

2 green onions (green part only), thinly sliced (optional)

1. In a large nonstick or cast-iron skillet over medium heat, melt the butter. Add the potatoes and cook for 12 to 15 minutes, turning them over about halfway through. Stir in the rosemary, cumin, chili powder, and salt.

2. Add the sausage into the mixture and stir to combine.

3. Make four wells in the potato-sausage mixture (you want to see the skillet underneath). Crack each egg into a spot. Cover, turn the heat to low, and cook until the egg whites are set, or 4 to 5 minutes.

4. Sprinkle the cheese and green onions (if using) over the top of the mixture.

5. Serve the eggs and potato-sausage mixture warm.

NOTES

- If you have uncooked sausage, simply add it to the pan with the potatoes in Step 1 to ensure it has plenty of time to cook through.

- During Step 1, you can make this Tex-Mex by replacing the rosemary with 1 teaspoon garlic powder as well as upping the chili powder and cumin to 1 teaspoon each. Garnish with fresh cilantro and sour cream.

- Make this with scrambled eggs by pushing the potatoes and sausage to the side of the skillet and cooking the eggs in the remaining space.

Add a veggie: In Step 2, stir 4 cups baby spinach into the potato-sausage mixture until it wilts and then add the eggs.

CHEESY CAULIFLOWER "RICE"

PREP TIME: 5 minutes

COOK TIME: 20 minutes

TOTAL TIME: 25 minutes

1½ cups uncooked jasmine rice or basmati rice

2 cups cauliflower "rice" (fresh or frozen)

½ cup shredded cheddar cheese

2 tablespoons unsalted butter

½ teaspoon garlic powder

¼ teaspoon fine sea salt

Sliced green onion (green part only), diced chicken, fried eggs, and diced tomatoes for topping (optional)

I'm not into pretending that veggies are grains, but I *am* into using veggies in all sorts of ways to help increase the odds that kids will enjoy them. And adding cauliflower "rice" to the pot with regular rice—because they cook at the same speed and blend seamlessly together—is excellent from both an ease and a flavor perspective. This vegetarian dish can be served as is or enhanced with all sorts of toppings. It also stores really well, so stash the leftovers in the fridge or freezer for a future meal.

1. In a medium saucepan, combine the jasmine rice and water to cover. Swirl and then drain off the cloudy water. Repeat the process another two times. This helps remove some of the starch on the rice.

2. Add 3 cups of water and the cauliflower "rice" to the rice in the pan. Set over medium heat, bring to a simmer, and cook for 12 to 15 minutes, or until the water is absorbed and the rice is tender. (If the water is absorbed but the rice is not tender, add a little more water, stir, and cook longer.)

3. Add the cheese, butter, garlic powder, and salt to the pan; stir to incorporate; and then turn off the heat.

4. Cover the rice and let sit for 5 minutes before serving with your choice of toppings.

NOTES

- If you use short-grain brown rice, increase the water to 4 cups.

- Use cauliflower florets, if desired; just mash up a little in the pot after the mixture is cooked.

Pick a protein: Stir in 2 cups diced, cooked chicken in Step 3.

BROCCOLI & CHEESE RICE CAKES

SERVES: 4 TO 6

PREP TIME: 5 minutes

COOK TIME: 16 minutes

TOTAL TIME: 21 minutes

2 cups cooked rice
(see page 239)

1 cup minced broccoli

1 cup shredded
cheddar cheese or
mozzarella cheese

2 eggs

1 teaspoon cumin

2 tablespoons unsalted
butter or olive oil

Salsa, sour cream, and
guacamole for dipping
(optional)

These tender rice patties have crisp edges and cook up in just a few minutes. They are a finger food for a casual-dinner night and are fun to dip in salsa, ketchup, or guacamole. I like to use leftover rice for this (so I make extra if I know this is on my meal plan later in the week) or you can use fully cooked rice from the store. Using kitchen scissors to cut off the tops of broccoli florets helps ensure that the pieces are small and cook quickly in the fritterlike cakes.

1. In a medium bowl, combine the rice, broccoli, cheese, eggs, and cumin. Using a fork, mix to form a uniform batter.

2. Set a large nonstick or cast-iron skillet over medium heat. Add 1 tablespoon of the butter. When the skillet is hot, add ¼-cup portions of the batter and, using a spatula, press down a little on each one to make a circle.

3. Cook the cakes for 3 to 4 minutes, carefully flip them, and continue to cook for 3 to 4 minutes more.

4. Transfer the cakes to a wire rack and repeat with the remaining butter and batter.

5. Serve the cakes, warm, with your choice of dipping sauces.

NOTES

• Try this with leftover cooked quinoa and an additional egg.

• Use cauliflower rice, shredded sweet potato, or grated carrot instead of the broccoli.

• Try Italian seasoning or pizza seasoning instead of the cumin to change the flavor.

FARRO–WHITE BEAN RISOTTO

Letting farro—a nutty, chewy wheat grain—simmer in stock and tomato sauce delivers a ton of cozy flavor without a lot of hands-on work. (To me, this tastes like a flavor mash-up of pasta fagioli and risotto, which is so yum!) We love this with white beans stirred in, though frozen peas would work too. Add sliced Italian bread and a salad on the side for a vegetarian family meal to share.

SERVES: 4 TO 6

PREP TIME: 10 minutes

COOK TIME: 33 minutes

TOTAL TIME: 43 minutes

2 tablespoons olive oil

1 shallot, peeled and minced

2 garlic cloves, minced

1½ cups farro, rinsed and drained

1 quart reduced-sodium vegetable stock

1 cup water

One 8-ounce can tomato sauce or marinara sauce

One 14.5-ounce can white beans (such as cannellini beans), drained and rinsed

¼ cup grated Parmesan cheese, plus more for sprinkling (optional)

½ teaspoon fine sea salt (optional)

Black pepper (optional)

1. In a wide skillet over medium heat, warm the olive oil. Add the shallot and garlic, stir to coat, and cook for 2 to 3 minutes, or until fragrant.

2. Stir the farro into the skillet, add the chicken stock and water, and turn the heat to high. When the mixture starts to boil, turn the heat to medium and let simmer for 20 to 25 minutes, stirring occasionally, or until the farro is just soft. (There may be a little stock left but it will be absorbed.)

3. Stir the tomato sauce, beans, and Parmesan into the farro. Turn off the heat, cover, and let sit for 5 minutes to warm through.

4. Serve the risotto sprinkled with the salt, pepper, and additional Parmesan, if desired.

NOTES

* Opt for the marinara sauce if you have one with a flavor that you love. (You can even add more than 8 ounces if you really love the flavor!)

* Use 2 cups frozen peas instead of the white beans.

Pick a protein: If it appeals to your family, add cooked, crumbled sausage on the side.

Add a veggie: In Step 3, stir in 1 pint halved cherry tomatoes for a burst of freshness.

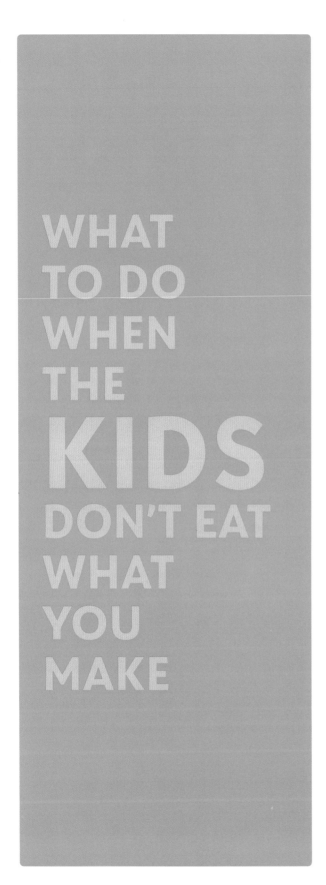

WHAT TO DO WHEN THE KIDS DON'T EAT WHAT YOU MAKE

The whole "but will they eat it?!" aspect of feeding kids is by far the hardest for me as a recipe developer and also just as a parent. Each of us is so unique—with our own specific food preferences and in different stages of learning to eat—that coming up with one meal for multiple people at the table can feel impossible. Or, at least, too often out of reach.

In many books, this is the place where the author promises the recipes at which you're looking will solve your problem. Unfortunately, it's not that simple. (I so wish it was!) Yes, what the kids will and won't eat has a lot to do with the actual food, of course, and there are ways to increase the likelihood that they'll eat a meal. But there are many other factors that have nothing to do with the food. Happily, adjusting these may be an easier way to improve mealtime dynamics.

Keep Preferences in Mind

Such adjustments can be as simple as using the shape of pasta they prefer; or if you know that they like to dip or dunk foods rather than use a spoon, letting them do that. If you know that the majority of the family doesn't like cauliflower, you might swap in broccoli. This is simply a reminder that no recipe is set in stone and you can always change a thing here or there to adapt it to your real-life people.

Make Sure It's Easy to Eat

For babies and younger toddlers, eating can be a really frustrating experience. The more we can try to cut food so it's easy to bite and chew, provide silverware that actually works (so many toddler forks are useless!), and help kids when you see them struggling at the table, the more likely it is that they'll enjoy their meal. Keep an eye out and offer help as needed.

Ditch Rules About "The Right Way" to Eat Foods

Kids have an intuitive sense of what tastes great to them and often combine foods that we think are super-gross. But honestly, who cares? If they want to put ketchup on something or mix together two things or pour their orange juice over their cereal—and they eat the food rather than just use this as a chance to play—I say, let them explore. You never know, they might come up with a combo that the rest of the family loves too. (The same is true if little kids still prefer to eat with their hands—it's okay if utensils take a while to get the hang of.)

Add Quick Sides

I say this a lot, but it's really okay to add simple sides to a meal when you're not sure if the kids will eat the main dish. That's not failing; it's ensuring that everyone has plenty to eat. (See page 115 for side-dish ideas.)

Know That Appetite Fluctuations Are Normal

No matter a person's age, it's normal for there to be days (or months) when appetite is up or down. So many of us are also hungrier at different times of the day than others. This means that the easiest way to know if a child is eating enough—even when it seems to us like they aren't—is to trust their hunger. And remember that intake balances out more over the course of a week than bite-by-bite at each meal.

Remember That No Two Plates Have to Look the Same

There's so much pressure to eat the same thing as our kids, but it's totally possible to make one meal and have it look different on each person's plate. Maybe one person likes their food mixed and another doesn't. One wants to top everything with basil or salsa or cheese, and another doesn't. Our plates can all be unique, even if we're starting with the same set of foods. That's normal and, frankly, to be expected.

Embrace a Boring Bedtime Snack

One of the easiest ways to take the pressure off of dinner—which is a time when everyone is often tired—is to have a boring bedtime snack option. That gives everyone a chance to eat something before bed if they're hungry. If the option is always the same and isn't super-exciting or a favorite food, then the kids are usually not inclined to skip dinner just to get the snack. In our house, we use a banana as the boring bedtime snack; we don't offer it, but the kids know they can ask for it on the way up to bed. Choose something that works for your family. (We landed on bananas because we usually have them and they are no-prep.)

MULTICOOKER MEALS

I know that many of us go through phases of loving one specific kitchen appliance or another, and while I don't think any of us needs a kitchen full of specialty appliances, I do think that a pressure cooker or a slow cooker should continually hold a top spot. These machines are so useful in low and slow cooking—we can get ingredients going in the morning and have dinner ready and waiting. They're also great for hot and fast cooking so that dinner can be ready in about 30 minutes from when we walk in the door. (No pot-watching required.)

Most of the following recipes have an option for either type of cooking so that you can use the multicooker you have or the one that works best for your schedule during any given week. (If a recipe only works in the Instant Pot and not the slow cooker, I give a stovetop or oven alternative.) The goal is to help you get dinner going but also keep you free to tend to the kids, feed the fish, or whatever needs doing. You can still pack in a lot of flavor without a lot of tending to the food while it cooks.

These are perfect for those nights when you really want a home-cooked meal but are low on energy (which I realize is maybe all nights!). Add a simple side (for ideas, see page 115), recruit the kids to help set the table, and enjoy.

CHANA MASALA WITH EXTRA VEGGIES

The sauce in this Indian-style dish is packed with veggies and flavor, and it coats the beans so nicely. To save chopping, you can swap in precut butternut squash from the produce aisle or use frozen diced sweet potato. (If using frozen veggies, the cook time will be about 10 minutes longer in the Instant Pot as it will take longer to warm up.) This doesn't taste exactly the same as the chana masala you'd get from an Indian restaurant, but it is a delicious home variation on the idea.

SERVES: 6 TO 8

PREP TIME: 10 minutes

COOK TIME: 10 minutes

REST TIME: 15 minutes

TOTAL TIME: 35 minutes

1 cup water

One 14.5-ounce can crushed tomatoes

4 cups peeled and diced sweet potato

2 garlic cloves, peeled

2 teaspoons cumin

1 teaspoon turmeric

1 teaspoon garam masala

½ teaspoon ground ginger

½ teaspoon fine sea salt

One 14.5-ounce can coconut milk (light or full fat)

Two 28-ounce cans chickpeas, drained and rinsed

2 cups cooked rice (see page 239)

Plain Greek yogurt, cucumbers, and/or naan or pita bread for serving (optional)

1. In the Instant Pot, combine the water, tomatoes, sweet potato, garlic, cumin, turmeric, garam masala, ginger, and salt and stir to incorporate.

2. Seal the lid of the Instant Pot and cook on HIGH pressure for 10 minutes. Naturally vent the steam for 5 minutes and then quick release to open.

3. Add the coconut milk to the pot and, using an immersion blender, puree to make a smooth sauce. Stir in the chickpeas and let sit for 5 minutes to warm through.

4. Serve the chana masala over the rice with yogurt, cucumbers, and naan, if desired.

NOTES

- Serve over pasta or couscous instead of rice, if your family prefers.

- Serve a little of the sauce with some bread as a dip, if the kids prefer it that way.

- Use fire-roasted tomatoes for a bit of extra heat and flavor.

SLOW-COOKER VERSION

In Step 2, cook on LOW for 6 to 7 hours or on HIGH for 4 to 5 hours. Continue as directed.

COCONUT CHICKEN & RICE

This is my favorite kind of dinner—dump everything into the Instant Pot or slow cooker and come back to loads of flavor! We like this tender shredded Indian-style chicken served over rice with diced cucumbers on top for a fresh crunch. Chicken thighs are great here, though you can use chicken breasts (boneless is better for ease) if you prefer.

SERVES: 4 TO 6

PREP TIME: 5 minutes

COOK TIME: 10 minutes

REST TIME: 20 minutes

TOTAL TIME: 35 minutes

1½ cups uncooked basmati rice

One 14.5-ounce can full-fat coconut milk

2 tablespoons garam masala

1 tablespoon cumin

½ teaspoon ginger

1 teaspoon fine sea salt

1 pound boneless, skinless chicken breast or thighs

1 medium cucumber, trimmed and diced

Naan bread and plain Greek yogurt for serving (optional)

1. Cook the rice according to the package directions, or until it is soft and most of the liquid has been absorbed. Turn off the heat, cover, and set aside.

2. Meanwhile, in the Instant Pot, combine the coconut milk, garam masala, cumin, ginger, and salt and stir to incorporate. Add the chicken to the pot, turning it to coat.

3. Seal the lid of the Instant Pot and cook on HIGH pressure for 8 minutes. Naturally vent the steam for 10 minutes.

4. Remove the lid from the Instant Pot and, using two forks, shred the chicken.

5. Serve the chicken over the rice with the cucumber, naan, and yogurt.

NOTES

- Use light coconut milk or coconut cream (if that's what is available at the store).
- Try pita bread instead of the naan.

SLOW-COOKER VERSION

In Step 3, cook on LOW for 8 hours or HIGH for 4 hours. Continue as directed.

Add a veggie: At the end of Step 4, stir 2 cups baby spinach into the shredded chicken. Let sit for 5 minutes to wilt and warm through

Make it vegetarian: Use two 14.5-ounce cans of drained and rinsed chickpeas instead of the chicken. In Step 3, decrease the cook time to 4 minutes.

BUTTER CHICKEN & RICE

PREP TIME: 10 minutes

COOK TIME: 10 minutes

REST TIME: 20 minutes

TOTAL TIME: 40 minutes

1½ cups uncooked rice

One 14.5-ounce can crushed tomatoes

2 garlic cloves, minced, or 1 teaspoon garlic powder

1 tablespoon freshly grated ginger, or ½ teaspoon ground ginger

1 teaspoon garam masala

1 teaspoon fine sea salt

1 pound boneless, skinless chicken thighs

2 tablespoons unsalted butter

2 cups frozen peas

Pita bread for serving

Sliced cucumbers and plain Greek yogurt for topping (optional)

Make it vegetarian: Use two 14.5-ounce cans of drained and rinsed chickpeas instead of the chicken.

This is one of my favorite chicken recipes to make for myself and to share with the kids. It's so flavorful from the mix of tomatoes, garlic, and spices. And it's a way to offer something a little unexpected without having to spend a fortune on ingredients that you may not use frequently. It can easily be doubled to make another full meal that you can stash in the freezer for a future night.

1. Cook the rice according to the package directions, or until it is soft and most of the liquid has been absorbed. Turn off the heat, cover, and set aside.

2. Meanwhile, in the Instant Pot, combine the tomatoes, garlic, ginger, garam masala, and salt. Add the chicken and stir to cover.

3. Seal the lid of the Instant Pot and cook on HIGH pressure for 10 minutes. Naturally vent the steam for at least 10 minutes. (It's okay if it sits longer, though.)

4. Remove the lid from the Instant Pot and, using two forks, shred the chicken. Stir in the butter and peas.

5. Serve the chicken over the rice with pita and your choice of toppings.

NOTES

- You can make the rice up to 5 days ahead or buy it fully cooked. I like jasmine rice here, but any kind you prefer will work.

- Feel free to use 2 pounds of chicken so you have more leftovers. The recipe works just as well.

- If you don't have garam masala on hand, use ground cumin instead.

SLOW-COOKER VERSION

In Step 3, cook on LOW for 7 to 8 hours or on HIGH for 3 to 4 hours. Continue as directed.

ITALIAN SHREDDED-CHICKEN SANDWICHES

The majority of the prep time in this recipe is for the Instant Pot to heat up. After that, it's super-fast, and you'll have shredded chicken ready for sandwiches in no time. The chicken is moist and flavorful (and so easy for little kids to chew) and it pairs nicely with a lot of flavors so you can add a variety of toppings, condiments, and spreads. We like these sandwiches in soft rolls (like brioche), though it would be delicious in Italian-style rolls too.

SERVES: 4 TO 6

PREP TIME: 10 minutes

COOK TIME: 10 minutes

REST TIME: 10 minutes

TOTAL TIME: 30 minutes

2 pounds boneless, skinless chicken thighs

½ cup reduced-sodium chicken stock

1 teaspoon Italian seasoning

½ teaspoon fine sea salt

½ teaspoon black pepper

½ teaspoon garlic powder

6 to 8 brioche or Italian-style rolls

Shredded lettuce, mayo, pickles, Thousand Island dressing, and ketchup for topping (optional)

1. In the Instant Pot, combine the chicken, chicken stock, Italian seasoning, salt, pepper, and garlic powder and stir to incorporate. Spread out the chicken so it's in a somewhat even layer.

2. Seal the lid of the Instant Pot and cook on HIGH pressure for 10 minutes. Manually vent the steam.

3. Remove the lid from the Instant Pot and, using two forks, shred the chicken. Pile the chicken onto the buns.

4. Serve the sandwiches with your choice of toppings.

NOTES

- We like this with a simple salad and a side of fruit. French fries or Roasted Potatoes (page 244) are great options too.

- Add hot sauce to your portion for more heat.

- Shred the chicken more finely for younger eaters so it's easy to chew.

SLOW-COOKER VERSION

In Step 2, cook on LOW for 7 to 8 hours or on HIGH for 4 to 5 hours.

SAUSAGE-POTATO SOUP

PREP TIME: 10 minutes

COOK TIME: 10 minutes

REST TIME: 10 minutes

TOTAL TIME: 30 minutes

1 pound uncooked mild Italian sausage links

1 cup peeled and diced carrot

1 cup diced celery

2 pounds baby Yukon gold potatoes, halved

1 quart reduced-sodium chicken stock

½ teaspoon Italian seasoning

½ teaspoon garlic powder

½ teaspoon fine sea salt

One 14.5-ounce can corn, drained and rinsed, or about 2 cups frozen sweet corn

1 cup sour cream or marinara sauce

Shredded cheddar cheese (to pair with sour cream) or grated Parmesan cheese (to pair with marinara sauce) for topping (optional)

This soup requires more chopping than most of the other recipes, but is one case where it is worth it. You can cut down on the prep by buying chopped mirepoix from the grocery store if your store carries it (look for it fresh in the produce aisle near other precut veggies or in the freezer aisle) and subbing it in for the carrots and onion. You can make this with either sour cream or marinara sauce—both are delicious and distinctly different flavor options.

1. Using kitchen shears, cut the sausage into bite-size rounds right into the Instant Pot. Add the carrot, celery, potatoes, chicken stock, Italian seasoning, garlic powder, and salt. (The stock won't quite cover the veggies—that's fine.)

2. Seal the lid of the Instant Pot and cook on HIGH pressure for 10 minutes. Manually vent the steam.

3. Stir the corn and sour cream *or* marinara sauce into the soup.

4. Serve the soup topped with your choice of cheese.

NOTES

- You can do all carrots and no celery if your family prefers that option.

- I leave the peel on the potatoes since the skin of Yukon golds is so thin. And it's nice to save that effort.

SLOW-COOKER VERSION

In Step 2, cook on LOW for 7 to 8 hours or HIGH for 3 to 4 hours. Continue as directed.

Make it vegetarian: Omit the sausage and add one 28-ounce can of white beans, drained and rinsed. Use vegetable stock instead of chicken. In Step 3, opt for the marinara sauce; it adds a depth of flavor you'd otherwise miss not using sausage.

BLACK BEAN– SWEET POTATO SOUP

This smooth, gently spiced black bean soup is a regular on our table. It can work as a big bowl, sure, but also as a dip if the kids are more apt to try it in a smaller portion. And the time it takes to make this recipe is primarily the time it takes for the Instant Pot to warm up—so you can do other things once you pop the ingredients in. I like to use frozen sweet potato here since it's already peeled and chopped, but you can start with fresh ones if you prefer. Orange juice is an unusual ingredient in a soup, I know, but it adds a sort of sweet, Moroccan-style flavor that's seriously yummy.

SERVES: 6 TO 8

PREP TIME: 10 minutes

COOK TIME: 8 minutes

REST TIME: 10 minutes

TOTAL TIME: 28 minutes

Two 28-ounce cans black beans, drained and rinsed

One 28-ounce can crushed tomatoes

One 14.5-ounce can reduced-sodium chicken stock or vegetable stock

One 10-ounce bag frozen sweet potatoes

1 cup mild salsa

Fine sea salt

½ cup orange juice

Shredded cheese, sour cream, tortilla strips, guacamole, and fresh avocado for topping (optional)

1. In the Instant Pot, combine the beans, tomatoes, chicken stock, sweet potatoes, salsa, and ½ teaspoon salt and stir to incorporate.

2. Seal the lid of the Instant Pot and cook on HIGH pressure for 8 minutes. Naturally or manually vent the steam.

3. Stir the orange juice into the Instant Pot and season with salt. Using an immersion blender, puree to your desired consistency. (You can also leave it chunky and skip pureeing.)

4. Serve the soup, warm, with your choice of toppings.

NOTES

- Start with super-small portions for kids who are still learning to like soup—and consider offering it as a dip for bread or crackers, which might be more appealing to them.

- Use pinto beans instead of black beans.

- Use butternut squash instead of sweet potato.

- To make this with fresh sweet potatoes, peel and dice two medium ones. Aim for about 2½ cups diced potato.

SLOW-COOKER VERSION

In Step 2, cook on LOW for 7 to 8 hours or on HIGH for 4 to 5 hours. Continue as directed.

VEGGIE BEAN CHILI

SERVES: 6 TO 8

PREP TIME: 10 minutes

COOK TIME: 10 minutes

REST TIME: 15 minutes

TOTAL TIME: 35 minutes

6 cups diced vegetables
(such as sweet potato,
butternut squash, onion,
celery, and/or carrot)

Two 28.5-ounce cans beans
(such as black, pinto,
or kidney), drained and
rinsed

One 28-ounce can
crushed tomatoes

One 14.5 ounce can
reduced-sodium vegetable
stock or chicken stock

1 tablespoon cumin

1 teaspoon garlic powder

1 teaspoon fine sea salt

One 16-ounce bag
frozen corn

¼ cup lime juice

Shredded cheese, sour
cream, avocado, cilantro,
and hot sauce for topping
(optional)

The beauty of this vegetable chili is that it's both versatile and quick to make—plus you have so many options for which veggies to use and how many shortcuts to take. I'm partial to using a mix of sweet potato and carrots with the beans, but I also love it with just precut butternut squash. See what you're in the mood for and don't forget the toppings . . . which in my house means *all* the cheese!

1. In the Instant Pot, combine the diced vegetables, beans, tomatoes, vegetable stock, cumin, garlic powder, and salt and stir to incorporate.

2. Seal the lid of the Instant Pot and cook on HIGH pressure for 10 minutes. Naturally or manually vent the steam.

3. Remove the lid from the Instant Pot and stir in the corn and lime juice. Let sit for 5 minutes to warm through.

4. Serve the chili with your choice of toppings.

NOTES

- This recipe makes a big batch of chili. Store leftovers in the fridge for up to 5 days and reheat for lunches throughout the week. Or you can freeze half of the batch for a future easy meal.

- Use canned corn if you prefer it to frozen. Just drain it in a colander and rinse it before adding it to the chili.

- You can add 1 tablespoon minced garlic, if desired, to add more flavor.

SLOW-COOKER VERSION

In Step 2, cook on LOW for 7 to 8 hours or on HIGH for 4 to 5 hours. Continue as directed.

PASTA & MEATBALL SOUP

Imagine the flavors of chicken noodle soup, but swap in meatballs for the chicken and you'll have an idea of what this tastes like. This soup is cozy, satisfying, and easy to adjust based on the amount of time (and energy) you have. You can use homemade meatballs or a favorite brand of frozen ones. I prefer mini meatballs since they're an easier size to eat with a spoon, but full-size ones can work too.

SERVES: 6 TO 8

PREP TIME: 10 minutes

COOK TIME: 15 minutes

REST TIME: 10 minutes

TOTAL TIME: 35 minutes

1 quart plus one 14.5-ounce can reduced-sodium chicken stock

1 cup diced carrots

1 cup diced celery

1 pound frozen mini meatballs or Homemade Mini Meatballs (page 216)

2 cups pastina, orzo or pearl couscous

8 ounces marinara sauce

Fine sea salt and black pepper

Grated Parmesan cheese for topping (optional)

1. In the Instant Pot, combine the chicken stock, carrots, celery, and meatballs.

2. Seal the lid of the Instant Pot and cook on HIGH pressure for 8 minutes. Manually vent the steam.

3. Turn the setting to SAUTÉ. Once the stock is simmering, add the pasta and cook for 5 to 7 minutes, or until just soft.

4. Stir the marinara sauce into the pasta to warm through and season with salt and pepper.

5. Serve the soup topped with Parmesan cheese, if desired.

NOTES

- You can use fully cooked rice instead of the pasta, if desired. Just stir it in and warm it through before serving.

- To vary the flavor, stir ¼ cup pesto into the pasta in place of the marinara sauce.

- Chop the carrots and celery up to 3 days ahead. Store in an airtight container in the fridge until ready to use.

- Use 2 cups fresh or frozen mirepoix so that you can skip chopping the celery and carrot yourself.

- Add more stock, as needed, when reheating the soup. The pasta tends to absorb it as it sits in the fridge.

SLOW-COOKER VERSION

In Step 2, cook on LOW for 7 to 8 hours or on HIGH for 4 to 5 hours. With the heat on HIGH, add the pasta and cook for 7 to 10 minutes, or until soft. Continue as directed.

HOMEMADE MINI MEATBALLS

MAKES: 1 POUND

1 pound ground beef

½ cup Italian-seasoned
  bread crumbs

½ cup grated
  Parmesan cheese

1 egg

½ teaspoon fine sea salt

Preheat the oven to 375°F. Coat a baking sheet with nonstick spray. In a large bowl, combine the beef, bread crumbs, Parmesan, egg, and salt. Roll into 1-tablespoon-size balls and place on the prepared baking sheet. Bake for 20 to 22 minutes, or until well browned. Transfer to an airtight container and store in the fridge for up to 5 days, or in the freezer for up to 6 months.

LEMON-CHICKEN NOODLE SOUP

Having a stash of frozen veggies in the freezer can save you so many minutes of chopping throughout the week—and makes for a colorful addition to this simple chicken soup. I prefer to use a pair of kitchen scissors to cut the chicken right into the pot . . . there's no cutting board to wash, and it's so much faster. Serve with a side of crackers and cheese.

SERVES: 6 TO 8

PREP TIME: 10 minutes

COOK TIME: 13 minutes

REST TIME: 10 minutes

TOTAL TIME: 33 minutes

1 pound chicken tenders or breast meat

2 quarts reduced-sodium chicken stock

One 10-ounce bag frozen mirepoix

2 bay leaves

1 teaspoon fine sea salt

1 pound "old-fashioned" egg noodles or egg tagliatelle

Juice from ½ lemon

Grated Parmesan cheese for topping (optional)

1. Using a pair of kitchen scissors, cut the chicken into bite-size pieces, dropping them right into the Instant Pot as you work. Add the chicken stock, mirepoix, bay leaves, and salt.

2. Seal the lid of the Instant Pot and cook on HIGH pressure for 8 minutes. Manually vent the steam. Discard the bay leaves.

3. Turn the setting to SAUTÉ, stir in the noodles, and cook for 8 to 10 minutes, or until tender. Then stir in the lemon juice.

4. Serve the soup topped with Parmesan cheese, if desired.

NOTES

- Double the chicken quantity if your family likes more meat.

- If you'd like to make this with fresh vegetables instead of the frozen mirepoix, use ½ cup each peeled and diced onion, celery, and carrot.

- To vary the flavor, use ½ cup pesto instead of lemon.

SLOW-COOKER VERSION

In Step 2, cook on LOW for 7 to 8 hours or on HIGH for 4 hours. Remove the lid and, with the heat on HIGH, add the noodles and cook for 5 to 10 minutes, or until soft.

EXTRA-VEGGIE MINESTRONE

Want minimal chopping but all the cozy flavors? This minestrone is better than it should be given how simple it is to throw together. Frozen veggies do the heavy lifting and provide a vegetarian soup that's big on taste but low on prep time. Serve with bread or cheese and crackers for a satisfying dinner.

SERVES: 6 TO 8

PREP TIME: 10 minutes

COOK TIME: 9 minutes

REST TIME: 10 minutes

TOTAL TIME: 29 minutes

1 pound ditalini pasta or elbow pasta

2 quarts reduced-sodium vegetable stock

2 tablespoons unsalted butter

One 14.5-ounce can marinara sauce

One 14.5-ounce can white cannellini beans, drained and rinsed

One 12-ounce bag frozen mixed vegetables (such as peas, carrots, green beans, and corn)

Fine sea salt

Grated Parmesan cheese for topping (optional)

1. In the Instant Pot, combine the pasta and vegetable stock.

2. Seal the Instant Pot lid and cook on HIGH pressure for 5 minutes. Manually vent the steam.

3. Turn the setting to SOUP to bring to a simmer. Add the butter, marinara sauce, beans, and mixed vegetables; stir; and cook for about 4 minutes, or until the vegetables are soft and warmed through. Season with salt.

4. Serve the minestrone topped with Parmesan, if desired.

NOTES

- To add extra flavor, sauté 2 garlic cloves (minced) in 2 tablespoons olive oil before adding the pasta and stock.

- Use chicken stock, if you prefer.

- Use a 12-ounce bag of frozen green beans instead of the mixed veggies, if you like.

STOVETOP VERSION

In a large pot over high heat, bring the stock to a simmer. Add the pasta and cook for 8 minutes. Then add the butter, vegetables, marinara sauce, and beans and let simmer for 4 minutes, or until the veggies are soft. Season with salt. Serve as directed.

RED LENTIL– COCONUT SOUP

With plant-based protein and subtle spices including ginger and turmeric, this vegetarian soup is cozy and comforting. It's also delicious either chunky or pureed smooth, so see what your family prefers. Note that this works best with red lentils, not brown or green ones (which take a lot longer to cook and have a stronger flavor). Pair with grilled cheese or crackers.

SERVES: 6 TO 8

PREP TIME: 10 minutes

COOK TIME: 15 minutes

REST TIME: 10 minutes

TOTAL TIME: 35 minutes

1 tablespoon coconut oil or butter

1 medium onion, peeled and diced

One 16-ounce bag shredded carrots, or 1 pound carrots, peeled and diced

1 pound frozen diced sweet potato, or fresh sweet potato, peeled and diced

1 teaspoon fine sea salt

1 teaspoon turmeric

1 teaspoon ground ginger

1 quart reduced-sodium vegetable stock

1 cup red lentils

One 14.5-ounce can full-fat coconut milk

1. Add the coconut oil to the Instant Pot and turn the setting to SAUTÉ. Once hot, add the onion, stir to coat, and cook for 3 minutes, or until the onion starts to turn a little translucent. Add the carrots, sweet potato, salt, turmeric, ginger, vegetable stock, and lentils.

2. Seal the lid of the Instant Pot and turn the setting to PRESSURE COOK and cook for 10 minutes. Manually vent the steam. Stir in the coconut milk. Leave as a chunky soup, if desired, or, using an immersion blender, puree to your preferred consistency.

3. Serve the soup warm.

NOTES

- Use 1 tablespoon freshly grated ginger instead of ground for more flavor, if desired.
- Use frozen diced onion to save on chopping.
- For tips on freezing and grating fresh ginger, see page 29.

STOVETOP VERSION

In a large pot over medium heat, warm the coconut oil. Add the onion, carrots, and sweet potato and stir to coat. Then add the salt, turmeric, and ginger and stir to coat. Cook for 5 to 8 minutes, or until the vegetables are just starting to soften. Add the vegetable stock and lentils and turn the heat to high. When the mixture boils, turn the heat to medium so it simmers and cook for 20 to 25 minutes, or until the vegetables are very soft and the lentils are broken down. Turn off the heat and stir in the coconut milk. Leave as is or puree if desired.

Sweet Potato Burrito Bowls, page 226

SWEET POTATO BURRITO BOWLS

Full of flavor and vegetarian comfort, these burrito bowls are great loaded with toppings that can be customized for each person in the family. We love them with fresh lime and sour cream, but you can also use the mix as a dip for tortilla chips or as a filling for tacos or burritos. This mix freezes really nicely, too, so stash those leftovers for a future meal. Photograph on pages 224–225

Photograph on pages 224–225

SERVES: 6 TO 8

PREP TIME: 10 minutes

COOK TIME: 10 minutes

REST TIME: 10 minutes

TOTAL TIME: 30 minutes

1 medium sweet potato, peeled and diced

1 cup reduced-sodium vegetable stock

One 28-ounce can black beans or pinto beans, drained and rinsed

One 16-ounce jar mild salsa

1 teaspoon cumin

½ teaspoon garlic powder

½ teaspoon fine sea salt

1 cup uncooked long-grain white rice

One 14.5-ounce can corn, drained and rinsed

½ cup shredded cheddar cheese

¼ cup cilantro (optional)

Tortilla or plantain chips for serving (optional)

1. In the Instant Pot, combine the sweet potato, vegetable stock, beans, salsa, cumin, garlic powder, and salt and then sprinkle the rice on top.

2. Seal the Instant Pot and cook on HIGH pressure for 10 minutes. Manually vent the steam. (If you're busy, it's okay to naturally release the pressure instead.) Stir in the corn and cheese.

3. Serve the bowls sprinkled with the cilantro and paired with the chips, if desired.

NOTES

- Use frozen sweet potato cubes instead of fresh sweet potato to save time. Or water instead of stock.

- Tortilla chips can be really hard to chew for kids under age 4, but you can offer a softer cracker, tortilla strips, or plantain chips.

- Wrap up the mix in tortillas to use as burrito filling.

STOVETOP VERSION

In a wide skillet over medium-low heat, combine the sweet potato, vegetable stock (increasing to 2½ cups), beans, salsa, cumin, garlic powder, and salt, then sprinkle in the rice. Bring to a simmer, cover, and cook for 15 to 20 minutes, or until the rice is tender and the liquid is absorbed. Stir in the corn and cheese and serve as directed.

MULTICOOKER MAC & CHEESE

I've made a lot of homemade mac and cheese over the years and I'm going to be honest: This is the only one all three of my kids like! We love it with broccoli stirred in at the end, though it's delicious plain too. It's creamiest right out of the pot, which is a great reason to get everyone to the table to dive right in.

SERVES: 6 TO 8

PREP TIME: 10 minutes

COOK TIME: 5 minutes

REST TIME: 15 minutes

TOTAL TIME: 30 minutes

1 pound elbow pasta

1 quart reduced-sodium chicken stock

2 tablespoons unsalted butter

½ teaspoon fine sea salt

½ teaspoon garlic powder (optional)

2 cups shredded cheddar cheese

1 cup shredded mozzarella cheese

1 cup milk

One 10-ounce bag frozen broccoli florets cooked according to package directions and drained (optional)

1. In the Instant Pot, combine the pasta and chicken stock.

2. Seal the lid of the Instant Pot and cook on HIGH pressure for 5 minutes. Manually vent the steam. Hit CANCEL to turn off the heat.

3. Stir the butter, salt, garlic powder (if using), cheddar, mozzarella, milk, and broccoli (if using) into the pasta. Cover for 5 minutes.

4. Serve the mac and cheese warm.

NOTES

- Use steamed fresh broccoli, if you prefer.

- Don't like broccoli? In Step 3, stir in 2 cups frozen peas as an alternative.

- Add sriracha or crushed red pepper to your bowl for a bit of heat.

- Serve with a side of fruit or a salad (but note that the milk and cheese make it pretty filling for a meatless meal).

STOVETOP VERSION

In a large saucepan over high heat, combine 2 cups milk and 1½ cups reduced-sodium chicken stock and bring just to a boil. Turn the heat to medium-high, stir in 8 ounces pasta and ½ teaspoon salt, and let simmer for 10 to 12 minutes, stirring occasionally, or until the pasta is just soft. Turn off the heat and stir in 1 cup shredded cheddar cheese (omit the mozzarella), a 10-ounce bag frozen broccoli, 1 tablespoon butter, and 1 tablespoon cream cheese. Season with salt before serving.

MULTICOOKER RISOTTO

I will never forget the holiday when I spent a full hour standing by a hot stove stirring risotto for my family. (I was also pregnant, so was sweating profusely by the end!) This version is so much less work, yet just as delicious.

SERVES: 6 TO 8

PREP TIME: 10 minutes

COOK TIME: 11 minutes

REST TIME: 15 minutes

TOTAL TIME: 36 minutes

2 tablespoons extra-virgin olive oil

1 medium yellow onion, diced

3 garlic cloves, minced

2 cups uncooked short-grained white rice (such as Arborio)

Fine sea salt

1 quart plus one 14.5-ounce can reduced-sodium chicken stock or vegetable stock

One 5-ounce bag baby spinach (optional)

½ cup freshly grated Parmesan cheese, plus more for serving

1 tablespoon unsalted butter

½ teaspoon finely grated lemon zest, plus juice from ½ lemon

1. Add the olive oil to the Instant Pot and turn the setting to SAUTÉ. Once hot, add the onion and garlic, stir to coat, and cook for 3 minutes, or until the onion starts to turn a little translucent. Add the rice and stir to coat, then stir in the salt and chicken stock.

2. Seal the lid of the Instant Pot, turn the setting to PRESSURE COOK, and set the timer for 6 minutes. Naturally vent the steam for 5 minutes and then turn off the cooker by hitting CANCEL. Manually release any remaining pressure. Stir in the spinach (if using), Parmesan, butter, lemon zest, and lemon juice.

3. Serve the risotto, warm, with additional Parmesan.

NOTES

- Use 2 cups frozen peas instead of the spinach, if you prefer.
- Use frozen diced onion and jarred minced garlic to make the prep time a little faster.
- Stir in ¼ cup pesto instead of the lemon juice to vary the flavor.

STOVETOP VERSION

Increase the broth to 2 quarts, place in a medium saucepan over medium heat, and bring to a simmer. Turn the heat to medium-low and let simmer. Meanwhile, in a large saucepan over medium heat, warm the olive oil. Add the onion and garlic to the oil, stir, and cook for 2 minutes, or until the onion is just starting to become translucent. Add the rice and stir to coat with the oil. Add 1 cup of the warm stock, stir, turn the heat to medium-low, and let simmer until the liquid is mostly absorbed. Repeat, adding 1 cup of the stock at a time until all of it is used and the rice is soft and cooked through. Stir in the spinach, Parmesan, butter, lemon zest, and lemon juice before serving.

GARLICKY SLOW-COOKED PORK

PREP TIME: 10 minutes

COOK TIME: 7 to 8 hours

TOTAL TIME: 7 to 8 hours, plus 10 minutes

5 to 6 pounds bone-in pork butt or shoulder

4 garlic cloves, peeled and minced, or 4 teaspoons jarred minced garlic

1 tablespoon crushed dried rosemary

1 tablespoon Dijon mustard

1 tablespoon olive oil

1 teaspoon fine sea salt

1 teaspoon cracked black pepper

It's great to top a cut of meat with just a few herbs and let it cook low and slow, especially on busy days and holidays when there's so much to manage in the house. Slow-roasted pork is festive and simple, so it works well for either occasion. I use pork butt, though you can also use pork shoulder—bone-in and boneless work about the same here. We like to have this with sliced whole-grain toast and a salad kit, though you could also serve it over noodles, if you prefer. It can sit on WARM for a few hours in the slow cooker if you need it to. Just be sure to spoon some of the liquid over the pork before serving to ensure that it's super-moist.

1. Place the pork into the vessel of a slow cooker.

2. In a small bowl, combine the garlic, rosemary, mustard, olive oil, salt, and pepper and stir to incorporate. Rub this mixture all over the top of the pork.

3. Cover the slow cooker with its lid and cook on LOW for 7 to 8 hours. (Check for doneness at 7 hours.)

4. Remove the lid, spoon some of the liquid over the pork, and slice or shred before serving.

NOTES

- You can make the herb mixture and rub it into the pork up to a day before you plan to cook it. Cover tightly and store in the fridge.

- If needed, shred the pork for little kids to make it easier to chew.

- Use a small chicken instead of the pork and proceed as directed.

OVEN VERSION

Preheat the oven to 325°F. Place the pork into a Dutch oven and coat with the combined garlic, rosemary, mustard, olive oil, salt, and pepper. Add 1½ cups reduced-sodium chicken stock, transfer to the oven, and cook for 3 hours. Check with an instant-read thermometer every 30 minutes until it registers 145°F. (It may take up to 4 hours to cook through.) Remove from the oven, spoon some of the liquid over the pork, and slice or shred before serving.

TIPS FOR HAPPIER FAMILY MEALS

I know firsthand how much pressure there is to have a family that eats a diverse range of foods as well as to make one meal that everyone will eat; a meal that everyone just sits down to without any fussing. But dinner often comes at the most challenging part of the day for kids—they are worn out and tired. Allow exposure to a range of foods to happen over time and remember that it usually takes most kids a while to learn to eat a wide range of foods. There is nothing wrong if your child doesn't eat everything. (And I bet you didn't eat everything you enjoy now when you were a kid!) So, while we may want to judge the success of a meal on who ate what, there are actually a lot of other factors to consider. Here are some of my favorite tips.

Focus on the "Why"

It's possible to remove some of the pressure on the "what" of meals and pay a little more attention to the "why." For example, your "why" for a dinner could be that it's a chance to connect with everyone after a day being apart, hear about how that math test went, share a new joke someone heard, or talk about an ongoing issue in the family. Or it might be a chance to fill a tummy before running off to soccer practice or art class. We don't always have to be checking off every single nutritional box for a meal to have value.

Talk About Other Things

When we sit down, I explain what foods are on the table (if I'm not sure my kids will know just by looks) and then we do our best to talk about other topics. This helps keep conversation free from verbal pressure to eat this or that, and it allows us to connect about other things. It also gives parents the freedom not to worry or keep tabs on what any one kid is eating or not eating so we can enjoy our own plate. I also find that my kids try more foods if they feel in charge of when, during the meal, they want to add something to their plate.

Add Music

For a while during 2020 and 2021, my family had what we called "fancy dinner night," which involved dressing up and putting on music to eat at our dining table. We still do it now, but usually we skip the fancy part and just add music—which is such a simple way to add fun (or calm, depending on what's needed) to a meal . . . especially when the kids are worn out from the day's activities.

Make Sure the Kids Are Comfy

There can be a lot of chaos at the table during the toddler years, and a lot of it may be related to whether a child is properly supported when eating. Aim for a seat that has support for their feet, is upright (like a highchair or sturdy toddler chair), and not reclined, or use a secure booster seat with a footstool underneath. Kids may not be able to sit at the table in a regular adult chair without endless squirming until they are much older.

Add a Side that the Kids Usually Like

One of my main goals with dinner is to be able to enjoy my plate without getting up seventeen times, so I try to put one or two foods on the table that the kids usually like—as safety nets. For our family, this is often milk and a side of fruit, though it could be anything. (See page 115 for more ideas.) If the kids don't love the main part of the meal, they can simply eat the sides. And I can stay seated.

QUICK & EASY SIDE DISHES

These simple recipes are the ones that I turn to over and over to round out a meal and can be made from a well-stocked pantry, fridge, freezer, and spice rack. They cover a mix of food groups, so you can add whichever ones you feel would make your meal better. Each can be paired with all sorts of other flavors.

PAN-SEARED CHICKEN TENDERS

This fast chicken recipe takes about 10 minutes and delivers moist, flavorful chicken without much work on your part. **SERVES 4 TO 6**

In a large skillet over medium heat, warm 2 tablespoons **olive oil** or **unsalted butter**. Add 1 pound **chicken tenders** and sprinkle with ¼ teaspoon **salt** and ¼ teaspoon **garlic powder** or **Italian seasoning** (optional). Cover the pan and cook for 4 minutes. Remove the cover, flip the chicken with a fork, and cook for 3 to 4 minutes more, or until the chicken is cooked through and the juices run clear. Serve with ketchup or any dipping sauce you like.

SEASONED BLACK BEANS

This is a simple side dish to pair with any Mexican-style meal or to add a filling side to ensure everyone has enough to eat. Some may like these beans topped with shredded cheese. **SERVES 6 TO 8**

In a colander, drain and rinse one 14.5-ounce can **black beans**. Transfer to a microwave-safe bowl and add 1 teaspoon **cumin**, ½ teaspoon **chili powder**, and ¼ teaspoon **salt**. Add ¼ cup smooth-style **salsa** (for additional flavor) and stir to mix. Microwave on full power for about 1 minute, stirring halfway through, and serve warm.

BUTTERED PASTA

Simple buttered pasta, while not the most sophisticated recipe in the world, is comforting and delicious. And it's a great option if you want a safety-net food choice on the table for the kids. **SERVES 6 TO 8**

Bring a large pot of **water** to a boil over high heat. Add 1 pound **pasta** and cook according to the package directions. (For the best al dente texture, I cook on the shorter end of the cooking range.) Using a ladle, reserve about ½ cup of the pasta water in a small bowl. Drain the pasta, return it to the pot, and add ¼ cup **unsalted butter** and one-fourth of the reserved cooking water. Stir a few times, adding more liquid as needed to coat the pasta with a glossy sauce. Serve with (a lot of) grated **Parmesan cheese**, if desired.

EASY STOVETOP RICE

I keep rice on hand to use as a base for many recipes because it's simple to cook, freezes easily (once it has been cooked and cooled), and there are so many varieties to choose from. This is a straightforward way to cook jasmine or basmati rice without having to stand and stir the pot. **MAKES ABOUT 3 CUPS**

Place 1½ cups **jasmine rice** or **basmati rice** in a medium saucepan. Cover the rice with water, swirling it and gently pouring it off (it will look a little white) to remove some of the starch. Repeat two or three times. Add 3 cups fresh **water** to the drained rice, set over high heat, and bring to a boil. Once it boils, turn off the heat, cover, and let sit for 20 minutes. Remove the lid (the liquid will be absorbed), fluff with a fork, and season with **salt** and **butter**, if desired, before serving.

SAUTÉED CARROTS

This is the carrot dish that I make most often in my house, and it's even better with a drizzle of honey, which enhances the natural sweetness of the veggie. **SERVES 4 TO 6**

Peel and trim 1 pound **carrots**. Cut the carrots into ¼-inch-thick rounds. In a medium skillet over medium heat, warm 2 tablespoons **unsalted butter** or **olive oil**. Add the carrots, stir to coat, cover the pan, and cook for 8 to 10 minutes, or until the carrots are very soft when poked with a knife. (If there's any liquid in the pan when you remove the cover, let cook for 1 or 2 minutes more to allow it to evaporate.) Drizzle with **honey** (optional, but recommended), sprinkle with a little **salt**, and serve warm.

NOTE

- Avoid honey for kids younger than one year old.

ROASTED CARROTS

You can call these "carrot fries" (pictured opposite) if you prefer and offer them with a side of ketchup. They're a great side for sandwiches, and the leftovers are delicious added to a salad or a lunchbox, straight out of the fridge. **SERVES 4 TO 6**

Preheat the oven to 400°F. Line a rimmed baking sheet with aluminum foil or parchment paper. Peel and trim 1 pound **carrots**. Slice the carrots into sticks about the length of your finger and the width of a pencil. (I usually cut each carrot into thirds, then cut each third into four sticks.) Place on the prepared baking sheet and toss with 1 tablespoon **olive oil**. Spread into an even layer and sprinkle with **salt**. Bake for 18 to 20 minutes, or until soft when poked with a knife. Serve warm.

AIR-FRYER VERSION

In a 375°F air fryer, cook for 10 to 12 minutes, or until lightly golden brown and soft when poked with a fork.

QUICK CHEESY SPINACH

Transform a bag of baby spinach into this delicious side dish in just minutes. You can also do this with baby kale or chopped full-size kale (stemmed), if you prefer. **SERVES 4**

Set a large skillet over medium heat. When hot, add 1 tablespoon **unsalted butter** or **olive oil**. Add 5 ounces **baby spinach**, cover, and cook for 2 minutes, Remove the cover, stir, and drizzle with the juice of half a **lemon**. Sprinkle with **salt** and shredded **cheddar cheese**.

BOILED BROCCOLI

This is, hands down, the broccoli method that I turn to whenever we have some that needs to be used up and I want it cooked quickly. The key? Be sure not to overcook it. (A timer can help!) **SERVES 4 TO 6**

Add a 16-ounce bag of **broccoli florets** to a medium saucepan, cover with water, set over high heat, and bring to a boil. Turn the heat to medium so the water simmers and cook for 6 to 8 minutes total (stir once after 3 to 4 minutes), or until the broccoli is soft when poked with a fork. Drain off the liquid, stir in 2 tablespoons **unsalted butter** or **olive oil** and sprinkle with **salt**. Serve with grated **Parmesan cheese** or freshly grated **lemon zest** for more flavor, if desired.

ROASTED BROCCOLI WITH PARMESAN

When my oldest went to daycare, the care provider there made this roasted broccoli that the kids went nuts for. There's just something about the slight caramelization and sprinkle of cheese that works so well. **SERVES 4 TO 6**

Preheat the oven to 400°F. Line a rimmed baking sheet with aluminum foil or parchment paper. Add 1 pound **broccoli florets** to the prepared baking sheet, toss with 2 tablespoons **olive oil**, and sprinkle with **salt**. Bake for 16 to 18 minutes, or until the broccoli is just tender and lightly brown. Remove from the oven, top with grated **Parmesan cheese**, if desired, and serve warm.

AIR-FRYER VERSION

In a 375°F air fryer, cook for 10 to 12 minutes, or until lightly golden brown and soft when poked with a fork. Top as directed.

ROASTED POTATOES

You can use full-size potatoes or baby ones in this recipe, but I prefer Yukon gold or a similar variety (and not a baking potato) for creamy insides and slightly crisp outsides. Do the spices on just half of the pan if they are too much for the kids. **SERVES 4 TO 6**

Preheat the oven to 425°F. Line a rimmed baking sheet with aluminum foil. Add 1 pound diced **Yukon gold** or **red-skinned potatoes** to the prepared baking sheet, toss with 2 tablespoons **olive oil**, and sprinkle with **salt**, crushed **rosemary**, **cumin**, and **chili powder**. Bake for 24 to 26 minutes, or until the potatoes are tender and have crispy edges. Remove from the oven and serve warm. (I recommend with ketchup!)

AIR-FRYER VERSION

In a 400°F air fryer, cook for 12 to 14 minutes, or until golden brown and cooked through.

STOVETOP RUSTIC MASHED POTATOES

A quick boil and a mash and you can have rustic mashed potatoes ready to share with the family. You can make these dairy-free if needed by using olive oil in place of the butter and a dairy-free sour cream. You can also make them super-smooth if you puree the mixture with an immersion blender. (I usually just leave them chunky since it's easier.) **SERVES 4 TO 6**

Add 1 pound diced **Yukon gold potatoes** to a medium saucepan, cover with 2 inches of water, set over medium-high heat, and bring to a simmer. Cook for 6 to 8 minutes, or until tender when poked with a fork. Drain off the water and return the potatoes to the pot. Add 2 tablespoons **unsalted butter**, ¼ cup **sour cream**, and a sprinkle of **salt** and mix and mash with a potato masher. Serve warm.

NOTE

- If you plan to puree the potatoes super-smooth, peel them to start.

SLOW-COOKER SWEET POTATOES

These taste just like baked sweet potatoes, only you can get the slow cooker going in the morning and forget about them until it's dinnertime. They're perfectly moist and can be quickly mashed with a fork once cooked.

SERVES 4 TO 6

Wash 4 medium **sweet potatoes** and, without drying them, place directly into the vessel of a slow cooker. Cook on LOW for 7 to 8 hours. Remove the lid, peel the potatoes, and place the flesh into a medium bowl. Mash the potatoes with a fork and stir in a little **unsalted butter**, if desired. Serve warm.

MAC & CHEESE BITES

This is a little "extra," but it's a fun way to serve a box of mac and cheese—and surprise the kids at the same time with handheld mac-and-cheese muffins.

MAKES 8 BITES

Preheat the oven to 400°F. Grease eight wells of a standard muffin pan. Prepare a box of **mac and cheese** according to the package directions. Stir in 1 **egg** and then place ¼ cup of the mixture in the prepared muffin wells. Sprinkle each with a little **cheddar cheese**. Bake for 10 to 12 minutes. Serve warm.

SAUTÉED CINNAMON APPLES

This is a perfect side dish (or snack) for a baby, but it's also so delicious at any age because it tastes like apple-pie filling. It pairs well with chicken or pork, though my kids eat it with anything! The leftovers are delish warmed or chilled too. **SERVES 4 TO 6**

Core and dice 4 medium **apples** (I leave the skins on). In a medium skillet over medium heat, warm 2 tablespoons **coconut oil** or **unsalted butter**. Add the apples and cook for 8 to 10 minutes, stirring occasionally, or until the apples are just soft but not falling apart. Serve warm, at room temperature, or chilled, sprinkled with **cinnamon**.

BAKED APPLE SLICES

Turn an apple into the yummiest of side dishes with this easy method. We eat these any time of the day. I love it as a simple way to use up any older apples lingering in the fridge—and the method works with pears too. **SERVES 4 TO 6**

Preheat the oven to 375°F. Place 1 tablespoon **unsalted butter** or **coconut oil** into a baking dish and pop it into the oven for about 1 minute to melt, then remove from the oven. Slice 4 **apples** into ½-inch-thick pieces (discard the core), put into the prepared dish, toss to coat, and sprinkle with **cinnamon**. Bake for 26 to 28 minutes, or until the slices are soft when poked with a fork. (Some varieties of apple may take longer than others to soften—Gala apple slices will cook a little faster than Granny Smith, for example.) Serve warm.

ACKNOWLEDGMENTS

This book has been in the making, in one form or another, since the day I became a parent. So thank you, sweet Linden, for making your opinions known right from the first time you sat in your highchair and inhaled roasted sweet potatoes. (And then mashed them all over the underside of the table.) Our family dinners have never been the same!

Tula and Selway, you have since joined in to keep me honest with your feedback. I am forever thankful for the endless willingness to taste-test my recipes—even when they haven't been your favorites.

To Josh, I love you and the life we've built together.

To Virginia Sole-Smith, Kate Tellers, Katherine Nolan Brown, and Liz Gilmore for keeping me sane through the ups and downs of life and motherhood. Virginia, I am forever grateful to you for helping me unravel diet culture and finding a more joyful pathway with food. (Also for always answering my 5:30 am texts.)

People often ask me how I got into cooking. It was from growing up in a family that was obsessed with food. Thank you for that, Mom and Dad (and all the grandparents who made it happen). And to Katie, Dave, and Andrew Gaines for sharing so many messy meals. A gigantic thank-you to John Melfi, Andrew Egan, and Jeff Snyder for always making me feel welcome and loved, especially when I was still figuring out who I was.

To everyone who has supported our family, from cleaning to childcare and backup childcare, you are so appreciated.

Thank you to Lauren Volo, Marcella Velasquez, and Maeve Sheridan for bringing the food in these pages to life with your gorgeous photography, food styling, and props. (And also for your flexibility in pivoting through the inevitable kid sickness that came up during the process.)

To the team at Rodale: Dervla Kelly, Phil Leung, Stephanie Huntwork, Jonathan Sung, Elisabeth Beller, Mary Cassells, and everyone who helped bring this book to market, thank you for your energy, ideas, and creativity. And to Lilly Ghahremani for your constant support.

Thank you to Laurie Buckle, Molly Benton, and Aurora Satler at Cookit Media for helping me to grow and thrive as a content creator. And to Madison Fitchl and Metta Cederdahl West, I appreciate your work behind the scenes at yummytoddlerfood.com more than I can ever say. (SO much!)

And to all of the readers and followers of YTF who have supported me over the years and are there each day to read my words and watch my videos—you are, quite simply, the best. I never could have dreamed that I'd be able to share my ideas and recipes with so many of your families and it's truly the greatest gift to have you all in my life. Thank you for trusting me to help you feed your people.

INDEX

ABOUT THE AUTHOR

Amy Palanjian is a content creator, recipe developer, and writer—and an (often tired) mama of three kids. She loves to help families relax about what kids are and aren't eating so that everyone can enjoy the benefits of being together at mealtimes. She knows that raising kids is hard enough without all the unrealistic pressure to raise "perfect eaters." You can find her recipes and daily doses of sanity-saving feeding content at her popular website, YummyToddlerFood .com, which is read by millions each month, and on social media: @yummytoddlerfood. Amy lives with her family near State College, Pennsylvania.